Cabrera Infante
in the
Menippean Tradition

Cabrera Infante in the Menippean Tradition

by

ARDIS L. NELSON

Florida State University

With a Prologue by

GUILLERMO CABRERA INFANTE

Juan de la Cuesta
Newark, Delaware

MANUFACTURED IN THE UNITED STATES OF AMERICA
Minimum pH of paper used: 7.0

ISBN (hardbound): 0-936388-15-3
ISBN (paperback): 0-936388-20-x
Library of Congress Catalogue Card Number: 82-082503

For Victor

TABLE OF CONTENTS

ACKNOWLEDGMENTS

I WOULD LIKE to express my gratitude to John P. Dyson, who first introduced me to *Tres Tristes Tigres*, and to Paulo de Carvalho-Neto, who encouraged me to send Cabrera Infante an early essay I had written on that book. This gesture, in turn, led to an epistolary friendship which has been a source of inspiration over the years. I wish to thank Guillermo Cabrera Infante for his kind permission to cite some of his letters, and I am especially honored by his contribution to this book of an essay, coincidentally an exemplar of Menippean satire.

I am also gratefully indebted to my colleagues and friends José Miguel Oviedo, Merle Simmons, Cathy Login Jrade, Miguel Enguídanos, Jane Maienschein and Marilyn Fowler, who read the manuscript at various stages and offered helpful advice toward its improvement. Acknowledgment is also due to my editor, whose suggestions and patience have been greatly appreciated.

Tallahassee
April 1983

«AVERTISSEMENT»
TO THE PROLOGUE

THE FOLLOWING "prologue" by Guillermo Cabrera Infante is no more a prologue than are his "novels" really novels. Here menippea parades as prologue, offering fresh wordplay, hyperbole and pun—a fitting introductory act for this book. In effect serving as an exact demonstration of Cabrera Infante's method of characterization, through stylization or imaginitive caricature, if you will, "A Portrait" is the mythification of a literary dialogue and a scholarly meeting at Yale, 16 April 1980, where I had been invited by Emir Rodríguez-Monegal to participate in "An Evening With Guillermo Cabrera Infante." The serio-comic spirit of Menippean satire is maintained throughout the piece you are about to read, even as Cabrera Infante lampoons writers, critics and academics.

A.L.N.

A Portrait of ARDIS
Reading my Books

By G. CABRERA INFANTE

por-trait (pōr'trāt, -trĭt), *n.* delineation of a person (formerly of any object).

The Oxford Dictionary of English Etymology,
ed. C. T. Onions

A portrait is the record of certain aspects of a particular human being as seen by another. The sitter may be deified or merely flattered by the artist, satirized or even maligned but, as long as some sense of individuality remains, a painting of him (or her) will be a portrait. The artist may be interested only in the sitter's physical appearance or social position or soul or unconscious, but again, as long as the sitter's identity remains, the artist will have painted his or her portrait. Finally the painter may paint him or her with a concern for precision of detail or with apparent abandon, with an interest in photographic realism or with a composition in Cuban. But still, whatever the style is, as long as the artist can suggest some aspect of a particular person, the work will be a portrait. (It may not be a very good portrait, but that is another problem.)

Encyclopaedia Britannica,
Vol. 18: PLASTICS to RAZZMATAZZ

Aʀᴅɪs ɪs Ardis Nelson, seen here sitting pretty. In fact she's one of those rare creatures who are undescribably beautiful. But as we're not going to have in this book her portrait by Sir Joshua Reynolds (among other reasons because Sir Joshua never painted it: it's all josh), I will attempt to describe her pen in hand. If you don't crowd in on me I promise I'll do my best. My best will always be everybody else's worst, I know. But then again that's the way all beauty crumbles.

This portrait in words is a poor substitute for an artist's master-strokes. (I know that too.) I believe, though, that every reader of this book must have at least a glimpse of its authoress to bathe their eyes in beauty prior to having before him or her the hideous subject of what can be fairly described as experiments *in anima viles.* As this experience will be a dissection (or my parts with art) each of you will have what Horatio in the fog gave Hamlet: "a piece of him." For the squeamish who hate dismemberments as a sideshow, you can have me whole in my books—one of them more than a whole a whale of a book, having the levity of a leviathan. In this vast volume I perform vivisection in different voices. In case you don't know, that's called ventriloquy: speaking from my belly. But let's go back to my American anatomist.

Actually Ardis is a radiant alien. At least that's how she looks standing next to me: I brown and brooding like a raisin pudding. Her radiance comes from her aura, unusually reflected by her complexion, fine and fair like a lemon and meringue pie. (I know, I know—this is beginning to look not like a beautiful friendship but rather like an American eatery. You wait and see: soon I'll be eating humble pie.) Her skin glows like the luminous frame illuminated books used to have in the Middle Ages and Ardis obviously belongs more in the library of the Duc de Berry than in mine, a paper-back reader. Her eyes that have read lucidly my clumsy words (including these, now seen by her for the first time, to her blushing astonishment, I'm sure) are of the stuff daydreams are made—but blue. A better artist than Sir Joshua—Hal Foster for instance—would have asked her to sit for him to draw from nature the ideal Aleta, that princess of the Misty Isles who lured so many horn-rimmed Vikings and then married Prince Val only because he looked like a Victor. With me, alas Aleta!, it's with words that you'll have to make do. Words and the eyes of a myopic beholder.

But now is her turn to do all the looking there is: a delicate girl turned by me into a Peeping Tom—with a little help from good old Gutenberg. She is that voyeur every reader must become to know a book better. In fact she has peered at mine with such intent that she has transformed me into a male Godiva made of chocolate. Reading Ms. Nelson aloud, from Ardis Nelson's book, this ogling opus, I felt like a clothesless child: so piercing, cutting so deep and so illuminating was the scrutiny she gave my pauper's pages clothed only in ragged words. She never—I repeat, never—committed the cruelty of crying out loud: "But this page is naked!"—making me into a figure of pun:

an infant without a paper diaper. But page or sage I suffered from what the French call *la pollution d'une page*. I must say, though, that she always had the gallantry of the really courteous and never read to reveal, in a literary kiss and tell. But, frankly, she told some. However, what she said was so penetrating that she placed her considerable (and considerate) intelligence at the service of the author, clothing me in her essays, as it were.

With the passing of time (Ardis by now believed I was an author for all seasons instead of fit to last only for the academic year) she corresponded with me in letters so Aristotelically ardent (remember that Aristotle and not Plato wrote the *Poetics*) that passionate friends would have never trusted them to a postman—or to the Pony Express for that matter. In her letters Ardis asked me the most intimate questions—all related to *Tres tristes tigres* and *La Habana Para un Infante Difunto*. She always knew that my answers were for her blue eyes only. Sometimes she thought my second best book was too much like the bed of an amateur Procustes. (I'm a leg man myself, mind you.) But I convinced her that compared with my books, so green, most blue movies were scarlet. She said that I sounded like Rimbaud—or was it like a rainbow? (How some of my mauve missives came to be trapped in this book like forgotten, fading flowers is still a mystery to me.) When she used my blue retorts to pinpoint a moot point never for a moment did she doubt my words on my words: that's high fidelity for you. But she always employed quotation marks as if to signal wayward readers that the inverted commas were a state of my deranged mind more than quotes. Any writer knows, or should know, that when he has such a prescient person for a scholiast he must forget that commentary is another name for hindsight. Art is total: that's how I pronounce Aristotle in Cuban.

There are two ways open to a writer to conduct a relationship with his critic. It's either love or hate at first sight. You don't even have to wait to see the white in a green-eyed critic's eyes to shoot him between the brows—either high or low. His writing (minus a t) will wring your neck from the printed page. Some critics are such artful dodgers in the vast field of literary ignorance that they deserve to be demoted to the rank of reviewer—which is the lowest form of the nitwit. There they'll do their usual write-ups: that's all they do. Under all reviewers roams the writer of *gacetillas* or copywriter. Some reviewers are beneath the copywriting stage, which is contempt. Others are constantly aspiring to the condition of critics—and thus we've come full circle. But between the critic and the deep blue sea of writing is the devil—sometimes only a devil's advocate. (Though a mere printer's devil would do.) Some writers, like me, use black ink instead of blue. Then the critic must face the black sea of writing from the beach at Odessa—always pronounced by him Odiousa. The critic sometimes collects debris here and there to make a bonfire of views: he is then, visibly beachcombing. But it's a well known fact that from the shipwreck of unsinkable literary liners many critics have made their notorious fortune: those are the professional scavengers posing as salvagers. Such is the case of F. R. Leavis and his wife (now made a widow by the critical establishment) and what was left of the *S. S. Dickens*, the ship that died of fame. Widow Leavis should move to Paris now and marry Lévy-Strauss and let their offspring (a bilingual critic no doubt) be called Leavis-Strauss. Then Junior could focus all his attention span (about ten minutes of it) on that couple of class comedians, Lawrence and Hardy.

Next come the quiet dons flowing calmly across Academia like blood vessels. These are the likes of Emir R. Monegal, Alfred MacAdam, and John Coleman, who though making a living as teachers are perceptive enough to be called critics. Besides, they are my friends. (If you notice that I repeat myself, don't adjust your sight: I've said this before.) But all is not brains that thinks in academic skulls. Once I was a guest at a Mid-Western university when I happened to remark that most campus critics smelled of *Toga Virilis*— even when it is worn by women. Scandal! How dare you, sir! See here, my good man! For a moment I thought I was back at Oxford. (Must I remind you that *Toga Virilis* is not an after-shave lotion?) Then, some time later, during my stay at a Southern outpost of progress, I scorched the earth like another Attila the Pun—the scourge of the Humanities. You see, I dared say that Galdós had a gall to call himself a writer. When I was leaving in a Dudgeon (the only decent means of transportation for a writer in which to leave a university) saying good-bye to the campus, I heard the burnt grass singing Garbo-like: "I want to be a lawn." (Not with my help, you won't.) To tell the truth, I don't care at all for those scholars whose most creative contribution to literary criticism is to scan some sonnets by Garcilaso or to teach American students that Berceo must be pronounced as in *birth* plus an expressive exclamation. Oh Henry! (Or I Married a Mad Medievalist from Madrid).

Of course that is not the case with Ardis Nelson—otherwise I wouldn't be talking you into reading her book, even if it is on me. Besides the special relationship we share (I write, she reads, she writes, I comment, she nods, she reads again then annotates) she has proved to have been for many years a serious student of my writings (which are usually not more serious than these facetiae) and a thorough teacher of what she has read. Sometimes, it's true, her American impotence of being earnest has killed some of my best jokes with critical kindness or a grave analysis, whichever comes first—though I suppose that the grave will come first. Compared to Ardis her colleagues, Professor Bergson and Dr. Freud, cracking jokes together, sound like a vaudeville duo (straight-men, no chasers). She has even seemed capable sometimes of making your regular Ibsen heroine look like a Carol Burnett of the *fjords*. (Fortunately she hasn't attained yet that stage of burning intensity an iceberg on fire called Hedda Gabler reached in mid-Winter, when she achieved spontaneous combustion. On the other hand it's also true that I haven't entrusted her with an unpublished manuscript of mine: my agent would disapprove strongly: "Remember Fahreinheit 451.") Some other times, I must admit, she has made light stuff of my heavy stuff, preventing it from becoming heady stuff in sentences running neck and neck with mine. (The end was usually a photo-finish—but more about photo-finish later.)

Like most writers (and perhaps more than most writers I know of) I write for myself. I don't sing to myself or even whistle as I stroll by, but I come close to patting myself on the back to say: "Well done, old boy!" I love to write and I enjoy reading myself. But not as much as other writers you don't know yet. Once Mario Vargas Llosa was flying down to Havana on a junket with a Spanish writer named Sol Sinsombra. In mid-flight Vargas overheard his fellow traveller giggle. Then he heard him laugh—loud, louder. As the now guffawing passenger was all by himself in the front seat, Vargas Llosa leaned over to see what the Spanish writer was laughing his head off about. It was a book, naturally. By straining, Mario Vargas was able to read the name above the title: unnaturally the Spanish reader was the Spanish writer. The man was laughing at his own jokes! Well, that could be me, you know. Except that I'm not Spanish and that I'd be smiling only. I cannot afford a laugh when I travel first class, even if the trip is paid by a foreign government.

I write for myself. To read what I've written I must then retype my material. I read myself again and the matter could rest there. I publish for the rest of you out there. Yes, you there on the other side of the page. For you and for you and for you. For all of you: to let you share with me the pleasure of my company. Perhaps the first writer to believe this and admit it in public was Oscar Wilde. But then Wilde admitted so many outrageous things in public—enough to scare the horse and the rider as well—that he shouldn't have been jailed for "posing as a *sondomite*" (whatever that is), as the Marquess of Queensberry accused him of, but for just posing. I never pose myself, least of all when I say I publish for the other. I like of course that my reader be capable of spelling my words right as I am of casting a spell with words in my writing. Many of my readers do. I can gladly announce that some of my readers can even read me without moving their lips—except women readers, of course. (I can tell instantly which readers are women: most moisten their lips as they read.) What I really hate is not for my readers not to know how to read me but that they might feel I am boring them. That's why I'm constantly asking the reader not if he's reading me but "Am I boring you?" With Ardis my perennial question (actually an ever-grin) has been: "Am I boring you arduously?" But Ardis has never been bored in my company. Nor in the company of my articles, or my letters either. (Even a telegram from me had her in stitches though not all of them could be blamed on me.) In turn I can swear I've never been bored with Ardis and I baptized her letters as Buenas Ardis (by Ardis mail). But now all I hope for is for Ardis to bore a full grove of academes with her book. Then, and only then, they'll find her book a good treatise. In Academia to read is not to fight a war of words but a truce in class.

Apart from many letters written by her to me (some left unanswered so far) there have been a few phone conversations in which Ardis artfully managed to hear with a gentle Van Gogh ear, my loud Gauguin-like manners on the mouthpiece. Sometimes she spoke so softly that before my answers reached her, her questions faded. In writing she tried to appease my teasing abruptness by suffering silently the blows of the Battling Kid Proquos of my ego. She even managed to follow my Non Sequi Tours in a taxi and took my quodlibet with a pinch of salt. (The worst remedy for those subtle arguments of mine is quod's libet oil. So a pinch of Ardis salt was not so bad a chaser after all.) Then came the lady in question in person to meet me in sections: a young lady that was actually a girl but very much like that blond boy the Cuban playwright Carlos Felipe described in his play *El travieso Jimmy*: "But what's that bright yellow thing shining in the middle of the square?" That's *un casque d'or*: the golden helmet of Ardis's *ardiente* hair burning brightly in the Connecticut light. And square was the only adjective to describe the other visiting professors surrounding her in the Yale campus during the Spring roll call.

Since then, since that Yale Spring morning in 1980, like Lewis Carroll with Alice in Oxford the Summer of 1865, it has been virtually (and virtue is the aching root here) impossible for me to judge Ardis (what she says, what she does, what she writes about my writings) impartially. This is a true confession: I'm always by her side—be that the sidewalk or an argument. All, as the last tango from Paris to Helen with love claims, "for a madding head." But the tango talks of a horse's head, a winning head—plus her golden hair. Take a bough, *Casco de Oro*. Atta Ardis! Now for an encore make me immortal with a book. Here it is!

This book has been dreamt in those Misty Isles that are the grey cells in what can be called the Ardis Head. That's not the name of a pub in Horatio Street like the Nelson's Head, but the blond head that should be placed not on a pedestal (that's a bust) but on the most prominent place of the book, the top of the spine—like a Celtic figurehead on a Viking vessel. The Norse custom has been suppressed in order to avert your eyes from the glowing head of Ardis. This will prevent you from being carried away (the way I do now) and ramble on about the authoress' glorious glare and rhapsodize on how a thing of beauty can be a Joyce forever—whistling in the dark to help you cross all puns asinorum like a bridge to Paronom Asia. Thus you can forget about the form fatale and concentrate on the content (as the malcontent rhetoricians used to say), which is the text. On the spur of the moment the prescient publishers wanted to print my likeness (or unlikeness, if you wish) not only on the cover but on the back cover too—under a convenient disguise. They asked me about a suitable mask for my *larvatus prodeo* and I retorted (I always retort): "What about a pun-name?" There and then they decided to publish my photo and be damn'd.

Now to eliminate the negative—which is this preface—and accentuate the positive—which is this book—all I can say to you is: *Tolle lege*. This is not a leg toll, but my Latinate way to invite you to a read. Come on in, by all means. But before you enter, do me a favour, will you? Clean your shoes on the doormat and please tread softly. Remember you are treading on my scholia.

London, Autumn 1982

Cabrera Infante
in the
Menippean Tradition

INTRODUCTION

GUILLERMO CABRERA INFANTE is one of the most popular contemporary Cuban novelists, along with Alejo Carpentier, José Lezama Lima, Severo Sarduy and Reinaldo Arenas. Carlos Fuentes says of his *Tres Tristes Tigres*: "Cabrera no es sólo el primer maestro latinoamericano de esa categoría central de la lengua inglesa, el pun o calambur... pero, al mismo tiempo, destruye la fatal tradición de univocidad de nuestra prosa."[1] David Gallagher cites *Tres Tristes Tigres*[2] as the most original and entertaining Latin American novel ever. While I agree with Gallagher, I hasten to add that although Cabrera Infante's works are unusual within the Latin American context, they are right at home when considered within the broader scheme of world literature. A great many characteristics of Cabrera Infante's works reflect the ancient literary tradition of Menippean satire, a serio-comic genre which arose from carnival attitudes. Menippean satire has been kept alive in the works of writers such as Varro, Lucian, Petronius, Apuleius, Rabelais and Sterne, and is emerging again today in the works of some of the new Spanish American novelists. Differing from our usual conception of satire, in which man's vices or follies are held up to ridicule with a decidedly moral or didactic purpose, Menippean satire is light-hearted and has no such moralistic end.

The most frequent questions asked of Cabrera Infante are those concerning the genre of his works *Tres Tristes Tigres* and *La Habana Para Un Infante Difunto*.[3] His denial that his books are novels is justified, for

---

[1] *La nueva novela hispanoamericana* (Mexico, 1969), p. 31.

[2] *Tres Tristes Tigres*, 4th ed. (Barcelona: Seix Barral, 1971). The title will be abbreviated *TTT* for page numbers in parentheses throughout the text, when necessary. Gallagher has a chapter on Cabrera Infante in his *Modern Latin American Literature* (New York: Oxford University Press, 1973).

[3] *La Habana Para Un Infante Difunto* (Barcelona: Seix Barral, 1979). The book's title will be abbreviated *La Habana* throughout the text.

it is my thesis that they are as much Menippean satire as novel.[4] It is with this view in mind, that I begin with a discussion of two important works from the Menippean tradition, the *Satyricon* and *Tristram Shandy*. Although there can be no doubt that other great works by authors such as Rabelais, Lewis Carroll and James Joyce have made a deep impression on Cabrera Infante, I have reason to believe that these particular literary works are the two which most influenced Cabrera Infante's creation of *Tres Tristes Tigres*. The Cuban author has said that Petronius' *Satyricon* is "the source of the book," and his narrators use many of the techniques used by Tristram Shandy in Sterne's work. A comparison of approaches used in creat-

[4] Recently a number of critics have been studying the question of genre in Cabrera Infante's narrative. Isabel Álvarez-Borland applies the theory of the short story cycle to all of his works up to *La Habana* in her practical inquiry *Discontinuidad y ruptura en G. Cabrera Infante* (Gaithersburg, Maryland: Ediciones Hispamérica, 1982). Emir Rodríguez-Monegal contends that Cabrera Infante's opus is autobigraphical in "Cabrera Infante: la novela como autobiografía total," *Revista Iberoamericana*, 47 (1981), 265-71.

A growing appreciation for the critical works of Mikhail Bakhtin (see note 10) is responsible, in part, for the concurrence of several scholars in their view of *Tres Tristes Tigres* as carnivalized literature. To my knowledge, I was the first to point out the presence of Menippean satire in Cabrera Infante in "Betrayal in *Tres tristes tigres* and Petronius' *Satyricon*," *Latin American Fiction Today: A Symposium*, Rose S. Minc, ed. (Takoma Park, Maryland: Ediciones Hispamérica, 1979), p. 154. While articles by M.-Pierrette Malcuzynski and Stephanie Merrim express ideological concerns and a concentration on language, respectively, the underlying premises of both critics support my thesis that Cabrera Infante is, in essence, a modern Menippean satirist. In her insightful study "*Tres tristes tigres*, or the Treacherous Play on Carnival," *Ideologies and Literature*, 3, No. 15 (1980), Malcuzynski argues that the notion of carnival plays a strictly formal, as opposed to subversive, role in *Tres Tristes Tigres*. Merrim in her excellent article "A Secret Idiom: The Grammar and Role of Language in *Tres Tristes Tigres*," *Latin American Literary Review*, 8, No. 16 (1980), 96-117, conducts a close analysis of the theme of language in each section of the novel, using Bakhtin's categories of dialogical *skaz*, stylization and parody.

Since the completion of this monograph I learned, through Merrim's article, that an unpublished, undergraduate thesis from Princeton University has been written on the concept of carnival in *Tres Tristes Tigres*: Antonio Prieto, "*Tres Tristes Tigres*: El carnaval de la palabra." Although I am not familiar with Prieto's thesis, it is more than likely that parallels exist between his study and mine, since Prieto also uses Bakhtin as a point of departure.

ing literary personages will serve well to highlight features of Menippean satire common to all three works. Some classical scholars, for example, believe that Petronius divides the personality of Nero among the characters of his work. Julio Matas has suggested that Cabrera Infante's three tigers represent the fragmented consciousness-memory of the author, that is, the division of one being into two or more characters.[5] And Sterne's work is, in effect, a fictive autobiography in which the author unfolds into the main character of his novel.

One of the most tangible differences between Menippean satire and the novel is characterization, which is defined, for the purposes of this study, as the means by which a writer attributes qualities or characteristics to the central figures of his literary composition. A character is usually a person, but it may also be language, a city or any fictional entity which serves as the central focus of the narrative. Critical concepts of characterization have changed greatly over the centuries. Aristotle, for example, saw it as a vehicle for demonstrating the moral qualities (goodness or badness) of man. E. M. Forster posits that we can know more about *homo fictus* than about our human acquaintances "because his creator and narrator are one."[6] Forster's view, however, is based on the omniscient, third person narrator. Nathalie Sarraute has a more contemporary insight into the use of the first person narrator, wherein the main character is referred to as "I": "[The reader] is obliged in order to identify the characters, to recognize them at once, like the author himself, from the inside."[7] Cabrera Infante's narrators are of this latter variety, requiring the reader to get involved.

Characterization as a feature of Menippean satire is contrasted with characterization in the novel by Northrop Frye, whose study I summarize here. While the novel is "extroverted" and "personal" and deals with men, their personalities and characters, Menippean satire is "extroverted" and "intellectual" and more concerned with mental attitudes or types of men, such as "pedants, bigots, cranks, parvenus,

---

[5] "Orden y Visión de *Tres Tristes Tigres*," *Revista Iberoamericana*, 40 (1974), 87-104.

[6] E. M. Forster, *Aspects of the Novel* (New York: Harcourt, 1927), p. 56.

[7] Nathalie Sarraute, *The Age of Suspicion: Essays on the Novel*, Trans. Maria Jolas (New York: George Braziller, 1963), p. 70.

virtuosi, enthusiasts, rapacious and incompetent professional men of all kinds" in terms of their "humor" or ruling passion. In the novel, characters tend to have *personae* or social masks, and are defined within a societal framework. Characters in Menippean satire are stylized, being representatives of a given set of ideas. While the novelist sees evil and folly as social diseases, the Menippean satirist sees them as diseases of the intellect and has traditionally ridiculed the *philosophus gloriosus*. The novelist essentially transfers theories to personal relationships, but the Menippean satirist intellectualizes and observes freely, often producing caricatures. While time and Western man are the materials for the novelist's creative treatment of history, the writer of Menippean satire presents "a vision of the world in terms of a single intellectual pattern," often by using the form of a "marvelous journey" or presenting "a caricature of a familiar society as the logical structure of an imaginary one," thus providing a distorted sort of unity. This tradition has been referred to variously as "loose-jointed," "chaotic" and "facetious," and its authors accused of "disorderly conduct." Sterne, as a disciple of Burton and Rabelais, was the first to combine successfully the novel with the "anatomy" (a term coined by Frye from Burton's *Anatomy of Melancholy*, as it reflects the intellectualized approach of Menippean satire). *Tristram Shandy* may be a novel, "but the digressing narrative, the catalogues, the stylizing of character along 'humor' lines, the marvelous journey of the great nose, the symposium discussions and the constant ridicule of philosophers and pedantic critics are all features that belong to the anatomy."[8]

Dorothy Gabe Coleman uses the term Menippean satire in her study of Rabelais "in a rather free sense to mean a mixture of verse interludes, or prose in different styles, parodies of epic, encyclopaedic erudition, serious episodes, humour and satirical criticism of topical events." She claims that "the most essential feature of the Latin Menippean satirists" was complete control by the author, for instance, Seneca's "authorial *I*" in his *Deification of Claudius the Clod*. Another basic narrative technique of the genre, in Coleman's estimation, was the imitation of writers as "a means of deriving irony, satire and humour." She focuses on three major traits of Menippean satire:

---

[8] Northrop Frye, "The Four Forms of Prose Fiction," *Hudson Review*, 2 (1949-50), 589-93.

parody, erudition and word-games, and satire. Similarly to Cabrera
Infante's brand of satire, the author finds that satire in Rabelais
serves to arouse pure laughter: "Comic and fantastic devices,... word
play... [and] the detachment of the author... leave the invective far
behind."[9]

In the critical works of Mikhail Bakhtin, we find a valuable
compendium of all the essential characteristics of the *menippea* (Bakhtin's preferred expression for Menippean satire) gleaned from his
study of antique Menippean satires. At this point I present his
unwieldy list, in schematic fashion, with an aim toward familiarizing
the reader with these unusual categories: a variable comic element,
"extraordinary freedom of philosophical invention and of invention
within the plot," the creation of "*extraordinary situations* in which to
provoke and test a philosophical idea... [T]he content of the menippea consists of the adventures of an *idea* or the *truth* in the world," the
combination of "free fantasy symbolism, and—on occasion—the mys-
tical-religious element, with extreme and... crude *underworld naturalism*," a genre of "ultimate questions," "threshold dialogs," "*experimental
fantasticality*," "moral-psychological experimentation," "artistic categories of the scandalous and the eccentric," "oxymoronic combinations,"
"social utopia... in the form of dreams or journies to unknown
lands," the use of other genres, "a new attitude to the word as the
material of literature," and a "topical and publicistic quality."[10]

The tendency in Menippean satire to devote an entire work to an
ideological issue provides the focus for the third and fourth chapters.
The idea of betrayal saturates every level of *Tres Tristes Tigres*, from
the fictional characters to the book's very existence. *La Habana*
similarly evokes the adventure of erotic love in all its phases, from
childhood, through adolescence, to adulthood. The city of Havana is
introduced as a central character in a book which purports to be a
"movie" of the erotic adventures of the first-person narrator.
Although the narrative is seemingly linear and consistently related by
the same character-narrator, the book is replete with elements of
Menippean satire. Both *Tres Tristes Tigres* and *La Habana* reflect the

    [9] Dorothy Gabe Coleman, *Rabelais: A Critical Study in Prose Fiction* (London:
Cambridge University Press, 1971). Quotes from pp. 85, 87, 89, 104.
    [10]   Mikhail Bakhtin, *Problems of Dostoevsky's Poetics*, Trans. R. W. Rotsel
(Ann Arbor: Ardis, 1973), pp. 92-97.

Menippean tradition through most of the above mentioned traits, but especially through characterization by "types," fragmentation or digression in the narrative, very little plot line and an all-pervasive comic element which runs the gamut from obscenity and the burlesque treatment of myth to erudition, word-play and literary parody.

Menippean satire transcends the personal preoccupations of novels through carnival attitudes such as *"free, familiar contact among people," "eccentricity," "carnivalistic mésalliances"* and *"profanation"* (Bakhtin, p. 101). When incorporated in literature, the revitalizing forces of carnival attitudes which celebrate perpetual change and renewal tend to imbue a work with an eternal quality. I believe that the wide appeal of Cabrera Infante's works can be attributed, in large part, to his return to the ancient Menippean tradition. *Tres Tristes Tigres* and *La Habana*, along with the *Satyricon* and *Tristram Shandy*, all exhibit a fortunate blend of menippea and novel.

1

Characterization in the *Satyricon*: A Model for *Tres Tristes Tigres*

SINCE THE FIRST TIME Cabrera Infante read Petronius' *Satyricon*[1] at the age of twelve or thirteen, the memory of this early prose fiction has haunted him. Having read the *Satyricon* many times over the years Cabrera Infante avows that the *Satyricon* is the "source" of *Tres Tristes Tigres*:

> La fuente del libro, ha contado Cabrera Infante, está en el *Satiricón* de Petronio: novela en la que de algún modo se capta la luz de la vela que alumbraba la decadencia romana y en la que también brilla el ingenio verbal, la libertad de las situaciones y la más sutil crítica social.[2]

Cabrera Infante further asserts that at times *Tres Tristes Tigres* tries to be a version of the *Satyricon*.[3] Alfred J. MacAdam has pointed out a basic similarity between the two works:

[1] The full name of the author is Titus Petronius Niger. He was known also by the title Arbiter of Elegance. All references to the *Satyricon* are from J. P. Sullivan's translation, Penguin Books, 1974.

[2] Emir Rodríguez-Monegal, "Estructura y significaciones de *Tres Tristes Tigres*," *Sur*, No. 320 (1969), 45.

[3] Alfred J. MacAdam, "*Tres Tristes Tigres*: El Vasto Fragmento," *Revista*

El mundo de *Tres Tristes Tigres* es estéril, a menos que se le
considere como origen de una obra de arte—de la misma
manera en que el mundo de Encolpio y Giton en el *Satiricón* es
un mundo que se revela como sin trascendencia (p. 556).

I

Interpretations of the *Satyricon* have varied widely, especially with
regard to characterization. A number of critics have put forth the
thesis that Petronius was satirizing Nero by dividing aspects of his
personality and life amongst several of the characters of the *Satyricon*.
This approach has been substantially discredited by more recent
research, but I wish to explore the earlier hypothesis, which was in
vogue until very recently, before going on to other views on
characterization in the *Satyricon*.

Gilbert Highet represents those critics who over the centuries
have chosen to view Petronius as a moralist satirizing Nero and his
entourage.[4] He considers the *Satyricon* an Epicurean satire, defining
satire as *ridentem dicere verum*, "telling the truth in a joke."[5] According
to Highet, the serious criticism in the *Satyricon* is based on Nero's
unofficial adventures and misadventures as recorded in the writings
of Juvenal, Suetonius, Tacitus and Philostratus. They provide historical evidence of nocturnal excursions enjoyed by Nero and the
noblemen of his court in which disguises, fights, robberies and
auctioning of stolen goods in the palace took place. Highet sees the
Satyricon in part as an imaginative record of these slumming trips on
which Petronius, who slept all day and devoted the night to busi-
ness and pleasure, must have led Nero. The emperor thought it
great fun to visit brothels and saloons disguised as a slave or soldier
while his companions robbed shops and insulted folks. Nero even
got into a fight once himself.[6]

Iberoamericana, 41 (1975), 552; In his interview with Emir Rodríguez-Monegal in "Fuentes de la narración," *Mundo Nuevo*, 25 (1968), 47, Cabrera
Infante says: "Siempre tuve el modelo de *El Satiricón*"; In Albert Bensoussan's "Entrevistas: Guillermo Cabrera Infante" (*Insula*, 286 [1970], 4),
he says: "*Tres Tristes Tigres* es...una traducción fallida del *Satiricón*."

    [4] His thesis is shared, for example, by Burman and Voltaire.

    [5] Gilbert Highet cites Horace's phrase in "Petronius the Moralist,"
Transactions of the American Philosophical Association, 72 (1941), 180.

    [6] Highet pp. 180-91. His observations are based on his reading of
Tacitus' *Annals*, 16.18.1 and 13.25, cited on pp. 189-90 of his article.

This type of activity is reflected in the characters of the *Satyricon* in such an extremely farcical way that Highet propounds the work as being exemplary of the Epicurean point of view of what should be avoided. Encolpius, the protagonist and narrator, along with his gang, is immersed in this kind of life most of the time, now being led to a brothel, now trying to sell a stolen cloak at dusk (12.1), now travelling in disguise on board a ship (103.3), often in fights to solve their personal affairs and always wandering aimlessly about. One night Encolpius is accosted by a shadowy figure who significantly might have been a soldier (82.2).

Richard H. Crum sums up other Neronian reminiscences in the *Satyricon*, found especially in some incidents occurring in the *Cena Trimalchionis* and in certain traits of Trimalchio which point to "a conscious, deliberate pasquinade upon the reigning prince, Nero."[7] Among the similarities between Trimalchio and Nero are, for example, their shared insistence on the colors scarlet and purple, the sporting of a large gold bracelet, an addiction to astrology and irrational beliefs, a distaste for philosophers, a love of the themes from the tragic stage, a passion for Homer, a delight in puns and a great love of music. At the banquet, mention is made of a water-organ accompaniment to a chariot race (36.7) which echoes a desire formerly expressed by Nero. The carver at the *Cena* has the same name as one of Nero's favorite slaves: Carpus. The fear inspired in the guests by the detachable ceiling laden with gifts (60.1-3) is an allusion to Nero's attempt to kill Agrippina by arranging to have a dislodged segment of the ceiling fall on her. A freedman at Trimalchio's banquet speaks of the evils of bathing, strangely reminiscent of Nero's having arbitrarily banished a man from Rome for having denounced the custom of bathing. Appearing after the *Cena* is another Petronian rogue, Eumolpus, one who is obsessed with reciting poetry on any and all occasions, and who, according to Crum's interpretation, explicitly parodies Nero's own rhapsody of Troy with his *Troiae halosis*.[8]

[7] Richard H. Crum, "Petronius and the Emperors; I: Allusions in the *Satyricon*," *Classical Weekly*, 45 (1952), 165.

[8] This paragraph is based on Crum's article, pp. 162-99. Crum's knowledge of Nero's idiosyncrasies comes from classical writers Suetonius, Tacitus and Philostratus, whose works he cites, pp. 163-65. It is interesting to note that Trimalchio's name is defined as meaning either "triply soft" or "great tycoon," p. 165.

The tendency of critics such as Highet and Crum to see the *Satyricon* as a derisive description of human folly, especially in the case of Nero, may well be influenced by our knowledge of Petronius' final act, his sending a list describing Nero's vices to Nero himself, without comment, followed by his breaking his own signet ring so that it could not be used by anyone else.

Opposing the view of the *Satyricon* as a satire on Nero is the theory that it was written expressly for Nero by someone who was on good terms with him. Originally suggested by Gaston Bossier in 1875, this thesis has been substantiated by recent scholarship on the date and author of the *Satyricon* and on the life and attitudes of Nero and his small artistic circle. Since the establishment of the date of composition at 64-65 A.D. coincides with the epoch in which Petronius was Nero's chosen Arbiter of Elegance, this thesis becomes especially plausible.[9]

Decidedly there are allusions to Nero and the times, but the very aspects of the *Satyricon* where scholars have found satire can be viewed just as well as providing amusement for Nero.[10] The title of the work itself is only mistakenly related explicitly to satire, as the word used is the Greek for "Satyr" and refers only to the erotic content.[11] All the areas of special concern to the Neronian circle are reflected in the *Satyricon*: poetic composition, which is variously represented and discussed (118); Greek art and culture, which are duly referred to; hostility toward Stoics, whose maxims are ridiculed (71.1); debauchery trips and sexual depravity, which are described in the characters' wanderings and promiscuity. That Nero heard and enjoyed the *Satyricon* is also verifiable by the presence of certain in-jokes which have been discovered in the text as well as by the loose, discursive structure of the work, suggesting a serial composition, well suited for episodic recitations (Rose, pp. 294-95).

Further light has been cast on Petronius' life and attitudes

[9] K. F. C. Rose dates the *Satyricon* in late 64 and early 65 A.D. in "The Petronian Inquisition: An Auto-Da-Fe," *Arion*, 5 (1966), 275-301.

[10] See Rose, pp. 295-98 for a thorough discussion of these aspects: vulgarity, gluttony, legacy-hunting, Roman administration in the Empire, Greeks, promiscuity, Stoics.

[11] Rose, pp. 291-92. Also J. P. Sullivan, *The Satyricon of Petronius: A Literary Study* (Bloomington: Indiana University Press, 1968), states that the original title of the work is *Satyricon libri (Book of Satyric Matters.)*

through a closer scrutiny of Tacitus' statements. In support of Petronius' friendship with Nero, there is good reason to believe that even after Tigellinus had brought charges of treason against him, Petronius preferred to remain in Nero's intimate circle rather than go into exile. As to the catalogue of vices he sent to Nero while dying, it was "a plain-spoken and ironic substitute ... for the usual fulsome adulation in wills of that time," entirely in keeping with Petronius' quality of *Species simplicitatis*, as mentioned by Tacitus (Rose, 290-91).

These investigations, then, have proven that the *Satyricon* is not a critical satire on Nero. But the *Satyricon* is within the Latin tradition of satire and its related genres, except for its " ... lack of a professedly moral or utilitarian standpoint," according to Sullivan. He further declares that "Petronius adopts its realism, defends it on Epicurean grounds; but he gives it a new and original function." The particular form within which Petronius chose to write gave him a great deal of freedom. Menippean satire is a narrative form dating from the third century B.C. which allows a mixture of prose and verse, as well as a temptation to literary self indulgence and formlessness. Significantly, parody and literary burlesque are a central feature of this genre. Petronius drew on Greek and Latin literary examples for use in many of the satiric and dramatic incidents in the *Satyricon*. The plot, for example, is loosely structured as a comic *Odyssey*, the *Cena* owes a great deal to Plato's *Symposium* and Horace's *Cena Nasidieni*, and the satiric subjects are traditional, including types such as legacy hunters, the high-born lady with a taste for slaves, importunant poets and reciters. Petronius' treatment of them, however, tends towards the novelistic, as his goal seems to be "a creative and humorous presentation of an imaginatively realized world."[12]

Another genre which Petronius puts to use is mime (*mimetic, imitative* of real life), an inferior but popular art form which concentrates on the lower side of life, observing in a somewhat stereotyped way everyday affairs and language, particularly those of the lower classes. Mime has similar aims to those of Petronius, according to his statement at 132.15 in the *Satyricon*: to narrate frankly the behavior of ordinary, i.e. inferior, people, and the

---

[12] This discussion is based on Sullivan. Quotes from pp. 89, 264.

pleasures of sex. Words, incidents and titles from mime appear in the *Satyricon*. Features common to mime and the *Satyricon* are colloquial speech, stock figures (like the go-between Chrysis), the *cineadus*, the excluded lover and themes of imposture and deception. "Mime subjects and situations provide the melodrama, the movement and incident for the picaresque plot and some of its farcial humour" (Sullivan, p. 223).

The use of low characters, along with cynical motivation and sexual situations, is a major aspect of satire which Petronius uses for his literary purposes. The way in which these characters are presented is also within the literary trends of Petronius' time. The connection between style and character was a main point of rhetorical theory to the Romans, for whom literature was meant to be read aloud. As we have only the written text and cannot know how variations in tone, pitch and tempo, as well as gestures which had specific functions, would affect the presentation, we can evaluate only the language that the characters use. There is a consensus among Petronian scholars that the characters in the *Satyricon* reveal themselves by their own words. From cultural standing to personality bents, individuality is established through linguistic patterns, phrases and topics. The clear distinction between the speech of the cultivated (Encolpius and his buddies) and the illiterate (Trimalchio and his freedmen friends) is unparalleled in Latin literature.[13]

In the *Satyricon* each character is a complex individual whose style of speaking is strictly in accordance with his personality. Let us take a brief look at some of the gallery of rogues. Giton, the young ex-slave who is the object of Encolpius' affections and jealousy, demonstrates a literary style in both his language and his behavior. His speeches, although literary, are artificial and self-conscious in tone. His style is declamatory, complete with excessive use of decorative alliteration and anaphora. He emphasizes the dramatic in speech and actions, and uses trivial epigrams which mirror his effeminacy

---

[13] Frank Frost Abbott, in "Use of Language as a means of Characterization in Petronius" (*Classical Philology*, 2 [1907], 44-49), gives examples of the frequency of the following colloquial elements in the dialogue lines of several characters at the *Cena*: certain vocabulary, pronunciation, word formation and inflectional forms typical of the uneducated.

and immaturity. Giton's bad rhetoric provides "platitudinous comments on absurd situations."[14]

In first century A.D. Rome, social class, as well as education, was demonstrated by one's use of language. Circe's maid, Chrysis, a slave who aspires to a higher social level than her own, avails herself of a more refined rhetorical style when she wishes to express disdain for men of her own rank.

Eumolpus, the immoral and opportunistic "sweet singer" (Sullivan, p. 227) of poems, is a vehicle for some of Petronius' literary views (p. 118). As opposed to Giton's vapid use of epigrams, Eumolpus' use of them is meaningful and witty, his literariness always bearing a functional relation to content, be it parodic or exemplary. Eumolpus is amusingly hypocritical, an inversion of Catullus' dictum that "a poet's life must be chaste, though his verses need not be" (George, p. 348). Eumolpus, the embodiment of a carnivalistic *mésalliance*, writes verse of a high moral quality, while his life is of the lowest. His style is terse, vivid and humorous, and, as his double nature provides equal amounts of vitality and refinement, he is the character perfectly suited to tell the two Milesian tales, whose "scabrous nature *plus* their literary history would be best suited by a style which is racy, and at the same time cultured" (George, p. 347).

Encolpius, Petronius' first person narrator and satiric vehicle, presents special problems for the critics. His style is imitative of whomever he is with, leading to psychological inconsistencies in his personality, which is very similar to Giton's. Both men are passive, submissive and suggestible, a compound of literary sophistication (although not in good taste) and practical naiveté. Both use declamations to express their literary pretensions, and both are imitative in style. Encolpius parrots Agamemnon in his use of metaphors and word-play, and in his hypocrisy.

Two basically different styles can be discerned in the ironic shifts of narrative focus. Encolpius, the timorous anti-hero and victim of the author's satire, displays an inferior rhetoric which appeals to the emotions. An analysis of his thoughts on death by

---

[14] This paragraph and the ensuing discussion of characterization by language is summarized from Peter George, "Style and Character in the *Satyricon*," *Arion*, 5 (1966), 337-55. Quote is from p. 343.

drowning (115) exposes Encolpius' style as being "complicated, verbose, ugly, and irrelevant.... The whole speech is a pompous procession of worn-out commonplaces, presented in the most trite rhetorical clothing. The exclamation, the imaginary objector, the paradoxes, the supposedly impressive generalization " (George, pp. 353-54). At times, however, the narration seems to be in Petronius' own style, since it appeals to the aesthetic sensibility and is at great variance with Encolpius' style. His description of the calm before the storm (109) is of the genre *descriptiuncula* (vignette) and gives the impression of easy perfection. As George notes, "The Latin is neat, graceful, and to the point. Special effects are used sparingly and economically" (p. 353). This ambiguity in the narrator's position, which could probably have been dispelled in performance, is Petronius' way of dissociating himself stylistically from the narrator in order to satirize him and the literary styles he voices.

While the individualization of the above-mentioned characters is most effective and detailed, the creation of Trimalchio, the ex-slave who has become a king in his own right, marks the pinnacle of Petronius' portrayal of a fictional character. As Sullivan posits, "He is dramatically presented from successive points of view, much as Socrates is presented in Plato's *Symposium*, and this is a true novelist's technique" (p. 265). His personality is revealed gradually, first through his physical surroundings, then by Encolpius' comments on him and the guests' conversations. External opinions are interspersed with Trimalchio's showmanship as a host, his anger at Fortunata, his reminiscing and his mock funeral. During the course of the banquet, Trimalchio's language and conduct gradually change, reflecting his increased intoxication. His dignity as a wealthy landowner finally gives way when he invites the cook and other slaves to join in the festivities. The changes in tone and points of view, the realistic details and dialogues, and the ironic reversals of the guests' expectations are all viewed as if by a disinterested and tolerant novelist.[15]

II

A review of the colorful characters in the *Satyricon* brings to mind numerous parallels with *Tres Tristes Tigres*. Since both works are propitious fusions of novel and menippea, the carnivalesque

---

[15] This paragraph presents Sullivan's interpretations, p. 265.

spirit pervades in all aspects we shall consider, from characterization to the treatment of themes in common, such as friendship, impotence and literary parody.

In ancient Rome the normal procedure for presenting a literary work was by oral recitation. Although such is not the case today, Cabrera Infante advises his reader that "la escritura no es más que un intento de atrapar la voz humana al vuelo," and suggests that "algunas páginas se deben oír mejor que se leen, y no sería mala idea leerlas en voz alta" (TTT, p. 9). Cabrera Infante has said that he wants to convert the spoken and written Cuban language into a valid literary language, and that he considers Tres Tristes Tigres "...una excursión al lenguaje."[16] Tres Tristes Tigres is a "gallery of voices," in which "la entonación, mímica y gestos sonoros desempeñan un papel de primer orden."[17] Behind each voice is an individual who presents him or herself in the first person. Although Encolpius serves as narrator of the Satyricon, each character is allowed his lines in the first person as well. While the motives of Petronius and Cabrera Infante may or may not coincide, both succeed in capturing in unprecedented clarity the linguistic patterns and mannerisms of various social classes and the regional dialects of their respective nations and epochs.

Critics have seen the introduction of characters in both works as cinematic. At the risk of being anachronistic, H. D. Rankin says of the Satyricon:

> Apart from the most prominent personae, characters in general...appear and disappear rapidly, almost as if they were flashed on to a screen. They are presented with what seems to be great economy, though the cinematic impression is enhanced by the broken nature of our text.[18]

Tres Tristes Tigres has often been referred to as fragmented and its characters tend to make brief and unexpected entrances, revealing themselves through dialogues, monologues, memories, music and rhythms. A glance through the expanded Index (See Chapter III)

[16] Emir Rodríguez-Monegal, "Las fuentes de la narración," Mundo Nuevo, 25 (1968), 45.

[17] Juan Goytisolo, "Lectura cervantina de Tres Tristes Tigres," Revista Iberoamericana, 42 (1976), 11.

[18] H. D. Rankin, Petronius the Artist (The Hague: Martinus Nijhoff, 1971), p. 12.

confirms the cinematic texture of *Tres Tristes Tigres*. "Los debutantes," for example, includes twelve fragments: seven vignettes (oral and written), the first two psychiatric sessions and the first three parts of La Estrella's story, "Ella cantaba boleros." A closer examination of "Seseribo" shows the seven fragments recounted by Ribot to be of a jumbled chronology. It is as if each section of *Tres Tristes Tigres* were a film cut edited without transition. The only long "take" is "Bachata," composed of twenty-three segments which are, for the most part, sequential. Given Cabrera Infante's background as a film critic, it is not surprising that many aspects of his novel seem to be more cinematic than novelistic in spirit and technique.[19]

The main character of both works can be seen as the society described therein. The first century B.C. was the epoch responsible for the formation of Nero, Petronius and his characters. In Rankin's words, "It was an age of great economic growth in the shadow of a principate which had struck root, and it produced patches of prosperity from which a number of individuals benefited to a vast degree" (p. 16). In effect, it was the age of Trimalchio. Through the individuals who make up the *Satyricon* we glimpse a vision of Roman society, characterized by "fluidity, untruthfulness, insecurity and ambivalence" (Rankin, p. 39). Similarly, *Tres Tristes Tigres* takes place during a period of affluence in Cuba in the late 1950's, an economic boom caused largely by tourism. Renowned for its casinos and entertainment, Havana rivaled Nero's Rome as a center of corruption and vice. The night life of Havana depicted in *Tres Tristes Tigres* symbolizes an era which Cabrera Infante wanted to capture in a book ever since he realized that those times were soon to disappear. The characters bring their differing ethnic and racial backgrounds to the city, whose night clubs, hotels, bars, apartments, cars and streets they inhabit and make their own, just as Petronius' characters frequent the mansion of a freedman who made good, the baths, the brothels, the rooming houses, the streets, marketplaces and ships, all of which typify the Neronian age. This interpretation of a city as a main character is borne out by Cué, "con su idea de que la ciudad no fue creada por el hombre, sino todo lo contrario" (*TTT*, p. 302).

---

[19] See my article on "*Tres Tristes Tigres* y el cine," *Kentucky Romance Quarterly*, 29, (1982), 391-404.

The *Satyricon* is often regarded as an "affectionate" parody of the *Odyssey* due to the abundance of allusions to Homer's work. The Wrath of Priapus from which Encolpius suffers is a humorous imitation of the Wrath of Poseidon.[20] Encolpius is a pathetic and absurd "Odysseus" with neither home nor destination. His "interior monologue" is reminiscent of "the egotistic objectivity of a Homeric hero describing what is happening within him, but with almost indulgent objectivity refraining from moral judgment on himself." Unlike the epic hero, Encolpius is shameless. Trimalchio, on the other hand, is "a person of heroic dimensions, whose only enemy is the inevitable death which he has tried to buy off .... Like a heroic character of epos, he is volatile and rude..." (Rankin, pp. 20, 27).

In *Tres Tristes Tigres* La Estrella is such a character. She may be considered the high point of Cabrera Infante's creation of a fictional character, as we shall see later on. As for some more specifically Homeric allusions in *Tres Tristes Tigres*, there is a bar named Laodicea, and references are made to "Sirens" and "Hades." Livia and Mirtila appear as sirens of the night, attempting to lure Silvestre and Cué up to their apartment. Also reminiscent of the sirens are Magalena when she is dripping wet (p. 57), Vivian at the pool (pp. 100-03) and "la ninfa hidrófila," the spouting statue (p. 412). Irenita "sirenita" and La Estrella are referred to as fish (pp. 62, 160), and La Estrella as a siren: "de su boca profesional salía el canto de las sirenas y nosotros, cada uno de su público, éramos Ulises amarrado al mástil de la barra" (p. 115). The night club below sidewalk level is described as an inferno (p. 277), and Silvestre returns home at the close of *Tres Tristes Tigres*.

While *Tres Tristes Tigres* cannot rightly be considered a parody of

---

[20] This view is elaborated in the following studies: E. Klebs, "Zur Composition von Petronius' Satirae," *Philologus* 47 (1889), 623-35; Rankin, pp. 19-21; J. P. Sullivan, *The Satyricon of Petronius: A Literary Study* (Bloomington: Indiana University Press, 1968), pp. 92, 93; J. F. Killeen, "James Joyce's Roman Prototype," *Comparative Literature*, 9 (1957), 193-203. Allusions to Homer's *Odyssey* can be found in the following sections of the *Satyricon*: 48, 97.5, 98.5, 101.7, all refer to the Cyclops theme; 105.9-10 burlesques Erycleia's identification of Odysseus (Homer, *Odyssey*, 19.473); 127.5 and 127.6-7 refer to Circe and Polyaenus (See Sullivan, p. 201, Note 11); 132.13 refers to Ulysses; 136.5-6, Encolpius kills a sacred goose, as Odysseus' men kill the Oxen of the Sun.

the *Odyssey*, it does partake of a literary tradition which goes back to the *Odyssey*, that of the symbolic journey. In the case of *Tres Tristes Tigres*, the journey is taken into the depths of Havana night life, where all the nights melt into one. Significantly, the first title which Cabrara Infante had selected for his story about La Estrella, which he considers the real beginnings of *Tres Tristes Tigres*, was *La noche es un hueco sin borde*. In novels such as Mark Twain's *Huckleberry Finn* and Conrad's *Heart of Darkness* the journey serves as both form and symbol:

> Their journeys penetrate into darker and darker and darker regions which correspond to states of mind and to conditions of man.... In such journey forms, the characters' voices are not crucial in moving the plot, for the "plot" is a pattern formed in the author's mind.[21]

In *Tres Tristes Tigres* there is little, if any, plot line in the traditional sense of the word. Its "gallery of voices" serves to amplify the narrator's memory of a certain time in his life as it coincided with an epoch in Havana.

In the *Satyricon* the relationship established between the author and the narrator is determined by the genre of the work and, as we have already seen, Petronius' use of the satiric mode is based on a literary impulse, as opposed to a moral one. Although authorial control is far from explicit in these works, both authors do make their presence known in a straightforward way, two times each, respectively. Petronius voices his literary opinions directly: in 118, through Eumolpus, showing his admiration for the traditional works of Homer, Vergil and Horace, and his condemnation of the contemporary Seneca and Lucan. In 132.15, through Encolpius, Petronius offers a poem which seems to be "a key to the whole work. It pleads for naturalism of attitude, language, and subject-matter."[22] The overall lack of identification between author and narrator lends an aura of impersonality to the work, which in turn may confuse the reader as to the author's intent.

Cabrera Infante's presence is indicated by his initials at the end

---

[21] C. C. Walcutt, *Man's Changing Mask* (Minneapolis: University of Minnesota Press, 1966), p. 92.

[22] See J. P. Sullivan's translation of the *Satyricon*, p. 197, Note 5, and p. 201, Note 21.

of the "Advertencia" and at the end of his note as chief editor of
Carteles to Silvestre (*TTT*, p. 439). While Cabrera Infante actually
held this post in Havana in 1957, in *Tres Tristes Tigres* it is Silvestre
who writes for this weekly publication, thus establishing a relationship of identity between author and narrator. Despite this point of
contact, which is tangential to the work as a whole, a tendency
towards detachment and its resultant complexity also occurs in *Tres
Tristes Tigres*. Elsewhere in the text Silvestre comments to Cué on
his role as writer: "Seré un escriba, otro anotador, el taquígrafo de
Dios, pero jamás tu Creador" (*TTT*, p. 408). For Juan Goytisolo this
character's self observation reflects and clarifies the novelist's role
as "no el narrador omnisciente a la manera del XIX, Jehová, Dios
creador."[23] Silvestre's role as narrator and creative writer will be
discussed in greater detail in the following chapters.

III

Several thematic lines run parallel in these works separated by
twenty centuries. Since the satiric mode traditionally included anything pertaining to popular entertainment, excepting competitive
athletics, it is not surprising to find folkloric elements in the
Satyricon. Petronius treats religious cults and popular superstitions
in a satirical manner. Of particular interest are the folk tales and
the Milesian tales: Niceros tells a werewolf tale at the banquet (61-
62) and Trimalchio relates an experience he has had with witches
(63).[24] The Milesian tale is a genre originated by Aristides of
Miletus (c. 100 B.C.) who wrote a number of popular erotic and
obscene tales called *Milesiaca*.[25] Eumolpus relates two of them in the
Satyricon, "The Pergamene Boy" (85-87) and "The Matron of Ephesus" (111-12).

Folklore is also an essential ingredient in the world Cabrera
Infante wishes to recapture in his fiction, as is noted by José
Schraibman: "Bustro representa el problema central que ha plan-
teado Cabrera Infante en su novela: la búsqueda del lenguaje que

---

[23] Goytisolo, p. 17. See also p. 15 for a comparison of the author/nar-
rator problem with the *Quijote*.

[24] See Anthony Rini, "Popular Superstitions in Petronius and Italian
Superstitions of To-Day," *Classical Weekly*, 22, No. 11 (1929), 83, 84.

[25] Philip B. Corbett, *Petronius* (New York: Twayne, 1970), p. 42.

capta la esencia de un pueblo, sus mitos, su folklore."[26] Beginning with its title, which is itself a popular tongue-twister, *Tres Tristes Tigres* provides an informal compendium of Cuban oral traditions. The children's nonsense song "Café" is duplicated in "Rompecabeza," that section of the book which epitomizes the continuous change which words, refrains and proverbs undergo as they are repeated over the years, ever-molded by the attitudes and opinions of the persons who utter them. Poems are parodied and refrains are jumbled. Códac says that Bustrófedon's oral literary parodies belong to folklore (*TTT*, p. 224). Another example is found in the first segment of "Seseribo" (*TTT*, pp. 89-90), a parodic description of the Rite of Sikán and Ekué from Afro-Cuban magic, indented as if it were a quotation. Seseribo is the secret and tabu drum (*tambor*) condemned to eternal silence because it is made from the skin of Sikán the Indiscreet, who caused the death of the sacred Ekué. Eribó is the new name given to the bongo-playing Ribot by Bustrófedon, thus linking the *zambo* with his racial and cultural roots.

The theme of impotence provides humor and may be symbolic in both works. Encolpius is afflicted with impotence as a result of his (unknown to us) offense against Priapus. He is impotent in all heterosexual and homosexual relationships except with Giton.[27] "Encolpius is the mouthpiece for the intellectual discontents of the age, and his sexual impotence itself might be taken as a symbol of the age's intellectual futility" (Rankin, p. 19). The women in the *Satyricon* are for the most part sexually menacing and contemptuous of males, the exceptions being Scintilla and Fortunata, wives of the rich freedmen Habinnas and Trimalchio. Quartilla, the priestess of Priapus, Tryphaena and the widow of Croton are sinister and ridiculous at the same time. Circe and Chrysis are cast in aggressive roles. Oenathea and Proselenus are lower priestesses who attempt to cure Encolpius' impotence in a demeaning and fearsome way. This presentation of women in a negative light is reflected as well in the weakness and treachery of "The Widow of Ephesus" tale.

In *Tres Tristes Tigres* we also find numerous frustrated sexual

---

[26] "Cabrera Infante, tras la búsqueda del lenguaje," *Insula*, 286 (1970), 15.

[27] The theme of impotence is found in the following parts of the *Satyricon*: 128.2,8-9, 129.5-7, 133.3, 134, 139.4 (probably), 140.11.

encounters and women who are either siren- or monster-like in some way. The male characters whom we see interacting with females are both attracted and repulsed by them. Cué and Silvestre, for instance, are physically attracted to Beba and Magalena, but are repulsed by their ignorance. Cué's unrealized love for Laura is thwarted by the wiles of Livia, one of the most interesting of the siren figures who, as in legends and in the *Odyssey*, seeks to entrap and destroy men. Livia uses her fashionable clothes and make-up to entice men up to her apartment (*TTT*, p. 143). She once lured Cué into her bedroom to show him nude photographs of herself, resulting in his loss of Laura as a potential lover (*TTT*, p. 152). Códac is strangely attracted to La Estrella. Although he is not physically desirous of her, she represents his ideal of all women in one, "a cosmic phenomenon."[28] In a more negative light, La Estrella is referred to as "la bestia" (p. 70), "La Ballena Negra" (p. 64), "un monstruo metafísico" (p. 281), and "mi pez enorme" (p. 160). Alex reports on La Estrella: "Su única debilidad, su solo aspecto humano son sus pies, no por la forma, sino porque le duelen, ya que los tiene planos, y se queja" (p. 84). Irenita too is seen as a fish, "otra criatura de la laguna negra" (p. 121), and has Cheshire cat-like qualities as well. Vivian is thought of as a thing, not a person: "es una máquina de escribir" (p. 109). Ingrid without her wig is Ionesco's Bald Soprano. Cué doesn't like the looks of Livia without her make-up and clothes, and Mirtila looks to him like "una mantis acorazada" (p. 155). The relationship between Beba and Magalena suggests a possibility of violence and lesbianism. It is all summed up when Silvestre says to Códac: "Pero no te rías tanto de Barnum, Beyle, que los dos traficamos con monstruos" (p. 168).

Friendship and betrayal are central themes in both Petronius and Cabrera Infante, and the underlying assumptions about these themes are strikingly similar.

> Friendship's a word and friends know its value—The counters slide merrily all through the game—Your friends broadly smiling, while fortune was by you: Their backs even broader when trouble came. *Satyricon*, 80

There is no real compassion amongst friends in the *Satyricon*. "In-

28 See William L. Siemens, "Women as Cosmic Phenomena in *Tres Tristes Tigres*," *Journal of Spanish Studies: Twentieth Century*, 3 (1975), 199-209.

deed, the tenor of the novel implies an attack upon the concept of friendship" (Rankin, p. 23). There is always an unstable love triangle, first with Ascyltos, Giton and Encolpius, and later with Eumolpus, Giton and Encolpius, involving jealousy, suicide threats or attempts and hysteria. These anomic figures are impulsive and self-centered, using others for their own immediate profit or pleasure. Several male characters in *Tres Tristes Tigres* are pals who enjoy punning with Bustrófedon and discussing women on a superficial level. But there is a lack of openness and trust between Cué and Silvestre, the two who spend by far the most time together, which implies that true friendship is impossible in the world of *Tres Tristes Tigres*, as it is in that of the *Satyricon*. The frustrated affair between Cué and Laura and the forthcoming marriage of Silvestre and Laura are forbidden topics during the long hours the two spend together. In fact, Silvestre's revelation that he will be marrying Laura seems to precipitate the end of the friendship.

One type of betrayal which exemplifies parallels between these two works is that of misleading others or deceiving one's senses through the wiles of pretence or falsification. According to Rankin, the *Cena Trimalchionis* is "a masterpiece of social pretence and bluff" (p. 41), the ambience of the banquet being an exhibitionistic display of the host's wealth and social status. The surprises experienced by Encolpius upon entering Trimalchio's house, in which almost everything turns out to be something different from what it first seems, is notably reminiscent of Cué's experience upon entering the house of the television celebrity in "Los debutantes." Both characters are betrayed by their senses in the entrance hall. Encolpius is frightened by painted watchdogs (29), while Arsenio comments on the unkempt young man beside him who turns out to be his own reflection in a mirror (*TTT*, p. 54).

Trimalchio's guests are repeatedly tricked into fearing for the well-being of slaves who are threatened with punishment for various offenses, when a sudden reversal proves it to be an ostentatious joke. The incident of the pig which the cook has supposedly forgotten to eviscerate is a good example. When the cook is about to be beaten, the pig bursts with a lavish outpouring of cooked meats and sausages resembling entrails. In *Tres Tristes Tigres* Cué proceeds into the TV celebrity's house where he too experiences uncertainty as to what is appearance and what is reality. This sequence is climaxed with a bluff worthy of Trimalchio: the wealthy host points a gun at Cué and shoots. Character and reader alike believe him to be dead, until the story is completed many pages later.

The *Satyricon* is ripe with all sorts of deceit and treachery, from such far-fetched cases as Quartilla's concealing her lust under the guise of malaria (16-25) to the rogues' disguising themselves as Ethopian slaves on board their enemy's ship (100).   Trimalchio's showmanship, which is self-aggrandizing and possibly a cover for his sense of inferiority dating back to his low beginnings in life, may be similar in its motivation to Silvestre's and Cué's punning and poeticizing to impress the girls they have picked up in "Bachata." Concealment of one's physical irregularities and emotional concerns are accepted behavioral patterns in *Tres Tristes Tigres*. The women wear make-up, and Vivian can tell her secret only to Eribó, a social inferior. Cué conceals his feelings even from himself and thus loses his only love. While in both works these themes help create an atmosphere of "apprehensive expectation," in Rankin's words, "a world in which nothing can be relied on, and nobody can be trusted" (pp. 50-51), in *Tres Tristes Tigres* the effect is multiplied indefinitely by the "author's" concealment of the plot from the reader.

Parody is an integral aspect of the carnival attitude and menippea. It is, in essence, "the creation of a *double which discrowns its counterpart*" (Bakhtin, p. 105). In both Petronius and Cabrera Infante literary parody is a major vehicle for comic effect.

The Arbiter of Elegance, "opposed to the glittering epigrammatic style of such contemporary authors as Seneca and Lucan," adapts and criticizes material from their works in a humorous way.[29] Lucan's *Pharsalia* and Seneca's *Moral Epistles* were being written and published contemporaneously with the *Satyricon's* composition. Although these authors are not mentioned by name, Chapters 118-24 clearly contain references to Lucan, for the criticisms therein could apply to no other work than the *Pharsalia*. Depending on the critic, Eumolpus' epic poem on the Civil War (119-24) is either a mockery, a parody or a travesty of Lucan's style. Eumolpus introduces the poem as unfinished and hastily prepared, thus

[29] *Satyricon*, p. 197, Note 5.

reflecting Lucan's notoriously speedy and extemporaneous writing. A comic effect is achieved by echoing Lucan's subject matter in different contexts. As opposed to Lucan, "Petronius, in accordance with the precepts of 118, carefully avoids anything resembling a scientific historical analysis."[30]

> For it is not historical fact that has to be handled in the poem—historians do this far better. No, the unfettered inspiration must be sent soaring through riddles and divine interventions and strange stories, driven by the weight of its language as though from a catapult, so that it gives the impression of prophetic ravings rather than the accuracy of a solemn speech before witnesses. *Satyricon*, 118

This brings us to the "Noticia" of *Tres Tristes Tigres* in which Cabrera Infante states that "Cualquier semejanza entre la literatura y la historia es accidental." This may not seem unusual for a twentieth century novelist, but Cabrera Infante's attitude is more emphatic than most: "Me interesa más la literatura que la historia. Prefiero una narración de mentiras *a priori* que una crónica de mentiras *a posteriori*" (Bensoussan, p. 4). While one of the main themes of *Tres Tristes Tigres* is its tirade on style and translation, one section of the book is strikingly similar in spirit to the *Satyricon's* literary parodies mentioned above: "La muerte de Trotsky referida por varios escritores cubanos, años después—o antes" (pp. 225-55). These parodies of Cuban authors have been transcribed by Códac from the tape recording made by the oral poet Bustrófedon. In them "'traduce' sus respectivas escrituras para ilustrar lo que habrían dicho si hubieran escrito sobre el asesinato de Trotsky."[31] Cabrera Infante's literary burlesque is made much more obvious by the use of the authors' names, and much more pointed by the intensive imitations of their styles, which Juan Goytisolo believes go too far (p. 14). Before a judgment is made on this issue, let us hark back to Petronius' flair for parody. In Rose's opinion, "Petronius' echoes are humorous and sometimes flippant" and his criticism

---

[30] This paragraph summarizes the relevant portions of Rose, on "Petronius and his Literary Contemporaries," pp. 61-74; also Appendix B: Adaptations of Lucan, pp. 87-93. Quote from p. 64.

[31] Suzanne Jill Levine, "La escritura como traducción: *Tres Tristes Tigres y una Cobra*," *Revista Iberoamericana*, 41 (1975), 559.

of Lucan is generally accepted as being intentionally "bad" criticism (p. 61). Some critics feel that Cabrera Infante's parodies are overdone, to the extent that they are more mocking than humorous. Nonetheless, when we consider that Bustrófedon wanted to create language and that he represents a total lack of respect for the written word, his parodies, similarly to Eumolpus', are consistent with his image as a character.

Along with Jorge Luis Borges, Cabrera Infante "ve la escritura como traducción" (Levine, p. 559). Written language is a transcription of the oral, which in turn is a transformation of the non-linguistic.[32] This process is so completely integrated into our cultural psyche that we are unaware of its taking place. Thus, in order to demonstrate that there is any process of transformation at all (that there is a radical difference between the linguistic and the non-linguistic, the verbal and the non-verbal), a parody of the familiar, at times brutal, is necessary.

In conclusion, both the *Satyricon* and *Tres Tristes Tigres* may be called comic novels, but it is, rather, those characteristics from Menippean satire which enable us to anlayze these works in a meaningful way. In the *Satyricon*, the *Cena* and the tale of the matron of Ephesus are considered to be pure Menippean satire. In *Tres Tristes Tigres*, "Bachata" has a similar function, as it takes the form of a symposium on wheels. Then, throughout the fragments of Petronius and the "fragmented" work of Cabrera Infante, the mixture of genres and styles, of high and low speech, of the incredible and the ordinary, all provide for the sudden reversals, the irony and the incongruity which is at the heart of the carnivalesque and Menippean satire. There is parody in the *Satyricon*, "particularly parody of those genres that depended upon or normally required oral presentation: epic, mime, tragedy, the rhetorical set-piece."[33] Cabrera

---

[32] Current models for understanding language hypothesize a non-linguistic conceptual structure; i.e., at a certain level human thought processes are believed to be language independent. For a more detailed account see R. C. Schank, *Conceptual Information Processing* (North Holland, 1975). This modeling stands in marked contrast to the Whorfian hypothesis about language and thought.

[33] William Arrowsmith, in the Introduction to his translation, *Petronius: The Satyricon* (New York: Mentor, 1959), p. x.

Infante's twist is to employ "oral" parodies of written works. Petronius' comic view, through Encolpius' narration, includes caricatures of all the types encountered, especially stuffy academics, rich businessmen and hypocritical poets. The same is true in *Tres Tristes Tigres*, where not only translators, artists and other types are caricatured, but the various character-narrators, as well, mock and are mocked in turn as the perspective shifts from one voice to another. *Tres Tristes Tigres*, as a book which tries to be a version of the *Satyricon*, clearly inherits the legacy of Menippean satire.

❧ 2 ❧

Of Hobby-Horses and Narrators:
Tristram Shandy
and *Tres Tristes Tigres*

 WELL-READ Cuban writer moves from Spain to England in the mid-1960's, while still working on the definitive version of his forthcoming book. Once settled in London, he chooses to read an eighteenth-century English work often considered a cornerstone in the development of the modern novel, *Tristram Shandy*. This is a possible scenario for Cabrera Infante's reading Sterne's book during the time he was actually writing *Tres Tristes Tigres*, a period during which the writer's sensibilities would be particularly sharpened. Sterne's late but profound influence on Cabrera Infante provides, in part, the rationale for dedicating a chapter to *Tristram Shandy*. More significant, however, is the enthusiasm shared by these authors for the same models from the Menippean tradition.

I

Since concepts such as genre and characterization develop within a cultural framework, a review of the philosophical and literary context from which *Tristram Shandy* emerged is apropos and enlightening as a background to our study of *Tres Tristes Tigres*. To begin with, Locke's *Essay Concerning the Human Understanding* (1690) was an important influence on Sterne, although just how it was utilized in his writing of *Tristram Shandy* is not at all clear. While some believe Sterne to be criticizing the Lockean thesis, others have gone so far as to consider Sterne the greatest exponent of Locke's theories in the eighteenth century.[1]

The medieval or scholastic view of perception, which went more or less unchallenged until the Lockean Revolution, held that men directly experience an objective reality outside themselves. Locke formed a new model of the mind which had an immeasurable impact on art and literature. His main hypotheses about human nature are that men cannot directly experience reality, but rather can know only their own subjective experience of that reality. These experiences take the form of ideas of which the "self" is conscious. Locke addresses the problem of identity, defining the "self" as "that conscious thinking thing, whatever substance made up of, (whether spiritual or material, simple or compounded, it matters not)—which is sensible or conscious of pleasure and pain, capable of happiness or misery, and so is concerned for itself, as far

---

[1] The latter view is held by Kenneth MacLean in his book *John Locke and English Literature of the Eighteenth Century* (New Haven: Yale University Press, 1936). John Laird, in *Philosophical Incursions into English Literature* (New York: Russell and Russell, 1962), pp. 84-88, describes Shandean philosophy as an elaborate application of Locke's methods, including an attempt by Sterne to improve upon Locke. A few of the many articles and books relating Locke and Sterne are Robert J. Griffin, "Tristram Shandy and Language," *College English*, 23 (1961-62), 108-12; Arthur H. Cash, "The Lockean Psychology of *Tristram Shandy*," *A Journal of English Literary History*, 22 (1955), 125-35; Ian Watt, "Realism and the Novel," *Essays in Criticism*, 2 (1952), 376-96; Carol A. Kyle, "A Note on Laurence Sterne and the Cannon-Bullet of John Locke," *Philological Quarterly*, 50, (1971), 672-74; D. W. Theobald, "Philosophy and Imagination: an Eighteenth-Century Example," *The Personalist*, 47 (1966), 315-27; Duke Maskell, "Locke and Sterne, or Can Philosophy Influence Literature?" *Essays in Criticism*, 23 (1973), 22-39; A. D. Nuttall, *A Common Sky: Philosophy and the Literary Imagination* (London: Chatto and Windus for Sussex University Press, 1974); Ernest Tuveson, *The Imagination as a Means of Grace: Locke and the Aesthetics of Romanticism* (Berkeley: University of California Press, 1960); John Traugott, *Tristram Shandy's World: Sterne's Philosophical Rhetoric* (Berkeley: University of California Press, 1954).

as that consciousness extends" (*Essay*... II, 27, 17). Hume carried Locke's theories to their logical conclusions. The split between objective reality and subjective experience led to Hume's assertion that only ideas, or bundles of perceptions, exist, and that there is no self and no objective reality.

Ian Watt sees the influence of this philosophical dualism in terms of literary realism, where there is a concern for the relation of the individual to his environment. The pretension of describing reality as apprehended by individual experience is characteristic of the novel form which tends, as does the general philosophical orientation of realism, to be "individualistic, critical, introspective, anti-traditional, and mainly concerned with eliciting truth from the evidence of particulars." The opposite poles of realism—subjective and objective—are not mutually exclusive, as "the most extreme subjectivists [in the novel] eventually place the individual in relation to the external world." Watt goes on to relate Sterne and Locke with regard to the dimensions of time, place and identity as experiential phenomena. "Our apprehension of time is an important psychological problem in Locke... [and] Sterne's treatment of time is the *reductio ad absurdum* of the philosophical-realist view of time." Besides having an external temporal realism in the historical sense, and an internal temporal realism in its narrative sequence of ideas issuing from the writer's mind, Tristram attempts to totally correlate the duration of fictional events with the reader's experience of them.[2] "Particular time and place combine in Locke to give the principle of individuation." In the novel, the character is individualized by a specific time and place, and the use of real names distinguishes the character of the novel from that of the romance. "Sterne takes the naming conventions of realism to their *reductio ad absurdum* by making the name Tristram Shandy the unique symbol of the bearer's destinies."[3]

Ernest Tuveson's summary of the general consequences of Locke's theories for literature, as seen in eighteenth century trends,

[2] See Theodore Baird, "The Time-Scheme of *Tristram Shandy* and a Source," *PMLA*, 51 (1936), 803-20.

[3] This paragraph is based on Ian Watt's "Realism and the Novel," *Essays in Criticism*, 2 (1952), 376-96. Quotes are from pp. 379, 380, 386, 388, 390, 391.

is also an apt comment on Sterne's approach to fiction. There is a shift of focus from the "actions of a character in a situation" to "reactions to a situation as it evolves." There is now an "interest in states of mind," in "impressions felt from within." "Character" becomes an acceptable theme in literature.[4]

Within his literary context, Sterne is not quite the revolutionary he is often believed to be. *Tristram Shandy* is really a unique blend of the old and the new. In Wayne C. Booth's estimation, "Sterne's true achievement is in taking forces which had become more and more disruptive in comic fiction and synthesizing them, with the help of older models, into a new kind of fictional whole."[5] Use of the self-conscious narrator in comic fiction before *Tristram Shandy* begins with the *Quijote*, although this device is not highly developed until well into the eighteenth century. The Arabic-speaking historiographer, Cid Hamet Benengeli, author (within the work itself) of the manuscript, is an intruding narrator, although the story he narrates is always related by the second narrator. While characters in both *Don Quijote* and *Tristram Shandy* comment on the story in which they appear, and in both the narrator expresses his awareness of himself as narrator, Tristram's conversations with a highly characterized reader go much beyond the intrusions in *Don Quijote*.[6] It is not until Marivaux (1688-1763) that the devices of intrusion in comic fiction are fully exploited, especially in *Pharsamon, ou les Folies Romanesques* (1737) and in *La Vie de Marianne* (1731-1741). In the *Pharasamon* and in *Tristram Shandy* one sees not only the narrator, his methods and physical surroundings characterized in great detail, but also the "readers." Booth points out some other elements in common, such as "reliance on chance, comparison of the book to a hazardous journey, suggested profundity beneath superficial folly, ... playful commentary on the relationship between duration in real

---

[4] Ernest Tuveson, "Locke and the Dissolution of the Ego," *Modern Philology*, 52 (1955), 169.

[5] Wayne C. Booth, "The Self-Conscious Narrator in Comic Fiction before *Tristram Shandy*," PMLA, 67, No. 2 (1952), 185.

[6] "...the device of the intruding narrator...had been used successfully by Cervantes, Scarron, Furetiére, and Congreve for comic ornament and for incidental parody of more serious writers. But their relatively skillful usage had little effect on comic writers generally" (Booth, p. 170).

life and in fiction" (pp. 172-73). *La Vie de Marianne* shares with *Tristram Shandy* "the use of elaborate delaying tactics before delivering promised material" (p. 174). In Marivaux's work, the heroine comments on her problems as a narrator, suggesting a device which Sterne carried to extremes: the book as product of its own subject matter. *Tristram Shandy* is the product of Tristram's character as portrayed in the novel.

Booth notes that there are striking similarities between Sterne's and Henry Fielding's narrative devices. In *Joseph Andrews* (1741) and *Tom Jones* (1749), Fielding uses a characterized, self-conscious narrator who intrudes and has discussions with the "reader." Novelists of the 1750's tended to copy these devices without regard to their artistic function. "The whole tendency throughout the fifties was really one of increasing disorganization, with ornamental intrusions used in ever more disruptive ways" (p. 176). While Tristram's intrusions on the one hand seem to be ornamental due to his claiming ignorance of how to proceed, they are actually "functional and carefully planned" (p. 177), although he presents this aspect much less often. As does Sterne, Fielding uses intrusions "to characterize the potential readers morally, and to manipulate the real readers into the moral attitudes" (p. 177) the author desires. Another function of this device is to insure "a comic response to scenes which in themselves are not necessarily comic, or which are even potentially serious" (p. 178).

Insofar as the role of the narrator is concerned, *Charlotte Summers* is an intermediary novel between those of Fielding and Sterne.[7] This work goes farther than Fielding "in the characterization of the 'readers,' in the intimate portrayal of the narrator in his physical surroundings, facing his writing problems, and in the elaboration of conversations between them" (Booth, p. 181). Sterne goes beyond *Charlotte Summers*, Booth avers, by "making his narrator the subject of his own book, and in extending intrusions in quantity" (p. 183) to the extent that the device becomes an end in itself, tranforming the nature of the work.

Sterne's discovery was the use of an intruding narrator to impose a new kind of unity, rather than that provided by plot, on

---

[7] *The History of Charlotte Summers, the Fortunate Parish Girl* (London, 1740), attributed to Sarah Fielding.

apparently divergent materials. The "older models" to which Booth
refers belong to that notoriously chaotic form of prose fiction called
Menippean satire, which we have already seen in Petonius and to
which the works of Burton, Rabelais, Swift, Voltaire and Erasmus
pertain. To what extent do we find echoes in *Tristram Shandy* of
these earlier literary models which partake of the Menippean tradition?[8] Both Rabelais and Burton introduce themselves in their
works, especially in prologues, epilogues and editorial comments.
Both digress, and in both the author's mind provides the shape and
pattern of the work. The Rabelaisian theme centers on narrow-
mindedness and hypocrisy in conventional thought-patterns, such
as the scholastic syllogisms. There is no plot. Similarly, in Burton,
the unifying topic is "melancholy." Works like Erasmus' *In Praise of
Folly* and Browne's *Vulgar Errors* "attempt to weld a great mass of
disparate material into a homogeneous whole" (Stedmond, p. 41),
while in *Tale of a Tub* Swift satirizes by adopting the mask or
position he is attacking and then revealing its weakness by ironic
exaggeration. Much of *Tristram Shandy* reflects traditional satire on
pedantry. The mock-serious use of learned footnotes, the presentation of an original document which is being discussed by the
characters and the appearance of an anonymous editor who points
out Tristram's errors (II,19) are but a few examples. Tristram is a
fully characterized narrator who provides a central point of view
and acts as an editor much of the time, often providing documents
and retelling anecdotes. Walter Shandy is an editorial commentator
at times (VI,31). This approach allows for the type of miscellaneous
erudition found in Menippean satire. But Sterne goes beyond his
precursors by weaving these scholarly tidbits into his narrative,
affirms Stedmond, "either by having them act as catalysts which
cause revealing reactions in his characters, or making them serve as
indicators of the texture of Tristram's mind" (p. 44). The later
models of Richardson, Fielding and Smollet provided, on the other

---

[8] The following discussion is based on John M. Stedmond, "Genre and
Tristram Shandy," *Philological Quarterly*, 38 (1959), 37-51. This and all subse-
quent articles by this author were later included in a single volume by the
same author: *The Comic Art of Laurence Sterne: Convention and Innovation in
"Tristram Shandy" and "A Sentimental Journey"* (Toronto: University of Toronto
Press, 1967).

hand, examples of novelistic techniques and a new way of handling such diverse material.

A number of Sterne's stylistic techniques which may strike today's reader as unique actually reflect the author's heritage and times. As Stedmond points out, his "conversational" style, techniques from the "anti-Ciceronian period," and a mixture of Cervantes and Rabelais and devices from the baroque aesthetic are all such elements.[9] Sterne's prose style was often admired for its oddity or individuality. Hazlitt called it "the pure essence of English conversational style."[10] Virginia Woolf praises the "jerky disconnected sentences" because they are "as rapid and it would seem as little under control as the phrases that fall from the lips of a brilliant talker." She admires the "very punctuation" because it is "that of speech, not writing, and brings the sounds and associations of the speaking voice in with it," and she finds that "The order of the ideas, their suddenness and irrelevancy, is more true to life than to literature."[11] But according to James Sutherland, most other eighteenth century prose stylists also had a "conversational" style.[12]

Sterne's diffuse sentence structure reflects the baroque "anti-Ciceronian" period of the seventeenth century, which Stedmond maintains was a reaction against formality of procedure and the rhetoric of the Renaissance schools, exemplified by two main types of style: the "curt" and the "loose." The *style coupé* features a "lack of syntactic connection between main clauses," and allows "the idea of the whole period [to be] contained in the first clause" followed by "a series of new expressions of the concept first stated" ("Style...," p. 245). Stedmond cites, as an excellent example of the curt period, Yorick's journey through his parish astride his horse: "Labour stood still as he pass'd,—the bucket hung suspended in the middle of the well,—the spinning-wheel forgot its round,—even chuck-farthing

---

[9] This section is based essentially on Stedmond's excellent article "Style and *Tristram Shandy*," *Modern Language Quarterly*, 20 (1959), 243-51.

[10] William Hazlitt, *Lectures on the English Comic Writers*, Vol. VI of *Complete Works of William Hazlitt* (London: J. M. Dent and Sons, Ltd., 1931), pp. 120-21.

[11] *The Common Reader, Second Series* (London, 1932), p. 79.

[12] "Some Aspects of Eighteenth-Century Prose," in *Essays on the Eighteenth Century Presented to David Nichol Smith* (Oxford, 1945), pp. 94-110.

and shuffle-cap themselves stood gaping till he had got out of sight..." (I,10). But the "loose" period is more typical of Sterne. It involves the use of "syntactic links, such as relative pronouns and subordinating conjunctions, which are, logically, strict and binding, to advance the idea, and yet, at the same time, it relaxes at will the tight construction which they seem to impose."[13]

> But I was begot and born to misfortunes;—for my poor mother, whether it was wind or water;—or a compound of both;—or neither;—or whether it was simply the mere swell of imagination and fancy in her;—or how far a strong wish and desire to have it so, might mislead her judgment;—in short, whether she was deceived or deceiving in this matter, it no way becomes me to decide (I, 15).

This seventeenth century style reflected a concern with the relation between thought and language, usually that of the author. Beginning with Sterne, the looser style became applied to the thoughts and language of fictional characters, as both Tristram and Walter Shandy use the anti-Ciceronian period. When the loose style is caricatured and all of its tendencies are carried to the extreme, the result is total confusion: "—and now, you see, I am lost myself!—"(VI, 33).

Among the English novelists of his time, Sterne alone succeeded in fusing the attitudes held by Rabelais and Cervantes towards language. Rabelaisian effects, for the most part externals of Sterne's style, occur mainly in passages attributed to Tristram, and help to individualize him as a character. For a brief summation of Rabelais' stylistic traits insightful to this study of Sterne and Cabrera Infante, I cite from Stedmond's article:

> *Gargantua and Pantagruel* is essentially an attempt to synthesize the world of obsolescent scholasticism, superstition, and chivalry with that of Renaissance humanism. In one sense it is an effort to explore the external limits of a rapidly expanding physical and intellectual world. The prose style ranges from the idiom of taproom chatter to the Ciceronian period. Rabelais takes every possible liberty with prose conventions; variations of word order,

---

[13] Stedmond, "Style..." pp. 245-46; Stedmond notes that this is the style of Bacon, the later Montaigne, La Mothe de Vayer, Sir Thomas Browne, the letters of Donne, Pascal's *Pensées*, in note 10, p. 246.

parallel lists of nouns or adjectives, repetitions, interruptions, parentheses. The bulk of the work is written in the colloquial manner; the rhythms are those of everyday speech. But the range of Rabelais' vocabulary is immense, and he delights in synonyms. Often he seems to prefer associating words by sound rather than sense, to begin with a scheme of word formation and then proceed almost mechanically. Sterne's verbatim borrowings from Ozell's Rabelais have often been noted, and they serve to illustrate the similarity between the manners of the two writers in such matters as the manufacture of names and words, lengthy word-catalogues, groupings of parallel words and constructions, ellipses, occasional inversions of word order, and so on. Both Sterne and Rabelais use language very self-consciously, like raconteurs who are also listeners to their own words. There is, however, in Sterne no sense of the autonomy of the word. His coinages are mainly playful, they are never exploratory thrusts into the unknown. In Rabelais, there is a sense of richness, of the renaissance urge to encompass all knowledge in its grasp. His use of language is generously expansive; Sterne's is critically selective.

Rabelais' style has been described as the orchestration of ideas: an idea is passed through two or more different vocabularies, as a musical theme is taken up by different instruments. Modern commentators on Cervantes have stressed what Spitzer calls his "perspectivistic" attitude toward his material. He uses words neither as an expansion of "life," like Rabelais, nor as depositories of "truth," like the medievalists (pp.247-48).

Using a device of the medieval etymologist, that of associating words by their homonymic relationships, Cervantes reveals the ambiguity of words when viewed from different perspectives. This is shown most clearly in the instability and variety of characters' names, in the clashing of socially based linguistic standards, in a tolerant attitude toward dialects and jargons and in a liking for puns. Stedmond considers language to be a character in its own right in Sterne's works, where we find an awareness of the relative nature of language, including ambiguities, double-entendres and puns, all of which emphasize the unstable nature of language. Postures, gestures and exclamations supplement and refine the meanings of words they accompany.

Sterne inherited many stylistic devices from the baroque aesthetic: "a predilection for 'polar mixtures,' for 'bold verbal figures' such as the pun and the paradox (double meanings in a word or phrase); the aposiopesis (meaningful silence); the apostrophe (digression to aid progression)" ("Style...," p. 250). Jefferson notes a suggestion of F. W. Bateson that the blank pages, wriggly lines, patterns of asterisks, etc., in *Tristam Shandy* may be a parody of the seventeenth century "shaped" poems.[14]

II

Although the Reverend Laurence Sterne presented *Tristram Shandy*[15] to the public as an anonymous work, the author soon became equated with his characters Tristam and Yorick. Sterne encouraged this identification and even conducted himself publicly as an extension of his book, to the extent that he was often called "Tristram." In spite of this practice, Laurence Sterne and Tristram Shandy are essentially different in character except that they are both writers who are witty and good-hearted. The character Parson Yorick has been seen as an idealized Sterne, as well as a jester. Introduced as the licenser of the midwife who was to be present at Tristram's birth, he is responsible, in a sense, for Tristram's "creation," just as Sterne is for the literary creation. Before the second installment of *Tristram Shandy* appeared, Sterne had identified himself with Yorick by publishing the *Sermons of Mr. Yorick*. While this character resembles Sterne in his professional role, he is removed from the scene early in the novel, helping to establish the autonomy of Tristram, narrator. The account of Yorick's death is separated from the subsequent chapters by two black pages, as if to emphasize its finality.

The complexity of the relationship between an author and his fictional world is expressed with regard to Sterne by an innovative critic, William V. Holtz. This writer considers Sterne-Tristram-Yorick-Walter-Toby "a protean creature," as "*Tristram Shandy* seems undeniably a complex and deeply personal extension of the man Sterne,

---

[14] D. W. Jefferson, "*Tristram Shandy* and the Tradition of Learned Wit," *Essays in Criticism*, I (1951), 237, note 1.

[15] Volumes I and II were published in December 1759 and 1760; Volumes III and IV in January 1761; Volumes V and VI in December 1761; Volumes VII and VIII in January 1765; Volume IX in January 1767.

a strategy for dealing with personal anxieties by transmuting them into art.... Tristram's story is fictional autobiography, while Sterne's becomes autobiographical fiction...in which Sterne's expanding objectification of his own identity rides on Tristram's effort to achieve the same goal."[16]

A fully characterized, self-conscious narrator born in 1718 (Sterne, in 1713), Tristram Shandy was thirty years old when Yorick died, and forty-one when he began writing his *Life and Opinions*. Tristram is a master of social discourse, his omnipresence unfolding into various roles: now and again minor character, editor, historian, autobiographer and author. All other characters and events pass through his mind, intermingling with his thoughts, as Tristram impersonates the actions and dialogues of the Shandy family he is immortalizing. Juggled throughout the nine volumes are two stories which Tristram wants to tell: that of his own childhood and that of Uncle Toby's courtship of the Widow Wadman. The latter is continually promised as his "choicest morsel."

Tristram's "life" is told in a most unusual way, the events of which compose his role as a minor character. Tristram's fortune and character seem to have been shaped by a sequence of unfortunate events, beginning with the circumstances of his begetting. It is not until Volume III of *Tristram Shandy* that we learn of a second misfortune, which involves the crushing of Tristram's nose at birth. This is followed by his misnaming at the christening and his accidental circumcision due to the fall of a sash-window. Considering that the book is about Tristram's life, we learn very little about him. Of Tristram's history we know only what the influences of the pre-natal period and early infancy have done for him which provides scant information from the point of view of the conventional historian or novelist. The "opinions" are those of the adult Tristram, autobiographer. An idea of their importance may be gleaned from the Greek motto from Epictetus which appears on the title page of *Tristram Shandy*, Volume I: "It is not things themselves that disturb men, but their judgments about these things." As an editor, Tristram makes an amusing compilation of the voluminous remains of Walter and Toby. He has an historian's concern for exact detail. Tristram, autobiog-

---

[16] *Image and Immortality: A Study of "Tristram Shandy"* (Providence: Brown University Press, 1970), pp. 144, 146.

rapher, uses satiric attitudes, rhetorical devices and stylistic traditons of older literature to reveal his subjective view of the world. As an author, Tristram is an artist attempting to produce an autobiography and a life. There is a "constant, curious, deliberate intermixture of Tristram's life with the narration of it,"[17] as if living and writing were part and parcel of the same thing.

This early psychological fiction has a modern ring. Wayne Booth perceives two aspects of Tristram's nature, "the ridiculous and the sympathetic."[18] He is ridiculous in his botched life and in his incompetency as a writer. As material for a traditional comic novel his stories could be told in quite a simple way, but chaos and complexity abound in *Tristram Shandy*. Tristram is sympathetic in his honest attempt to get at the inner reality of his life and opinions. In so doing, he shares the obstacles that confront all men: the elusiveness of truth and time, the unpredictability of the mind and the intrusion of human animality on our more lofty goals. As Tristram tries to find himself, he seems rather to lose himself. Thus, he feels he must write about the process of writing about himself, all of which results in further loss of self.

Although Tristram often makes abrupt transitions from narration to direct address to the reader (VI, 10, for example), from fiction to the awareness that this is fiction, Ian Watt envisions Tristram's narrative voice as the one thing that is consistent in *Tristram Shandy*. His prose style "embodies the multiplicity of his narrative point of view," and is effected by an unconventional use of punctuation, especially the dash, which is "invaluable for enacting the drama of inhibited impulse, of the sudden interruptions and oscillations of thought and feeling, which characterize Tristram both as person and as narrator."[19]

Tristram is quite explicit in his desire to communicate with his readers:

[17] Juliet McMaster, "Experience to Expression: Thematic Character Contrasts in *Tristram Shandy*," *Modern Language Quarterly*, 32 (1971), 54.

[18] This paragraph summarizes Booth's discussion in *The Rhetoric of Fiction* (Chicago: University of Chicago Press, 1961), p. 230-33.

[19] Ian Watt, "The Comic Syntax of *Tristram Shandy*," in *Studies in Criticism and Aesthetics 1660-1800*, eds. Howard Anderson and John S. Shea (Minneapolis: University of Minnesota Press, 1967), p. 321.

I have undertaken, you see, to write not only my life, but my
opinions also; hoping and expecting that your knowledge of my
character, and of what kind of mortal I am, by the one, would
give you a better relish for the other: As you proceed further
with me, the slight acquaintance which is now betwixt us, will
grow into familiarity; and that, unless one of us is in fault, will
terminate in friendship—*O diem praeclarum!*—then nothing which
has touched me will be thought trifling in its nature, or tedious
in its telling (I, 6).

When we listen to the narrative voice as if it were conversation, it
becomes clear that the main dialogue of *Tristram Shandy* is actually
between Tristram and the reader, at least half of the book being
direct address to the audience, often about matters tangential to the
story. Tristram's self-consciousness is "other-directed" for his primary concern is to train and educate the reader's imagination in an
attempt to make the reading public at large more discriminating.[20] In
an analysis of this relationship, Howard Anderson points out three
devices which Tristram uses to encourage us to be better readers and
happier people: his unconventional narrative form, "parables of preconception," and *double-entendres.* By choosing "to turn his misfortunes
into high comic art" in a most unusual way, Tristram "gets us to
reconsider what a narrative (and a life) is."[21]

Tristram addresses specific readers directly. Eugenius and Garrick
are real-life friends, while Jenny is imaginary, as are the anonymous
others such as "Sir Critick," "dear Madam" and "fair reader." He
exploits the audience's tendency to identify, by characterizing the
reader he is addressing as dull, hostile, lascivious and so on. Tristram
forces the reader either to become involved or put the book aside.
Since the reader's expectations of what narrative form should be are
deliberately and continually disappointed, William Bowman Piper
suggests that he experiences a series of changes in attitude—from
doubt, to embarrassment, to defensiveness. Not only do the many
digressions frustrate the reader's desire to know what will happen
next, but they can also infuriate him, as nearly all are directed at the

[20] See John M. Stedmond, "Satire and *Tristram Shandy,*" *Studies in English Literature,* 1 (1961), 55-57.

[21] Howard Anderson, "*Tristram Shandy* and the Reader's Imagination," *PMLA,* 86 (1971), 968-69.

audience, for purposes of explanation, instruction or amusement.[22]

Yorick's story provides a "parable of preconception" in pointing out the human predilection to think the worst of others whenever possible. Just as the parishioners gossip about Yorick and unjustly snub his honest supportiveness, we are annoyed by Tristram's jokes at our expense, even though we have benefited fom his truly generous motives, as have the country folk from Yorick's. Through the example of false judgment of Yorick's character, Tristram guides the reader towards a more favorable opinion of the narrator. Anderson's view is that "if our patience and trust can prevail over our laziness, skepticism and lack of humour, perhaps we can benefit, along with jests and jibes, from our association with Tristram" (p. 971).

Anderson interprets Tristram's *double-entendres* as "a primer in poetry." First we see how easy it is for prurient interests to cause us to jump to conclusions on very little evidence. We grow more and more uncertain as Tristram repeatedly assures us that his meaning of "nose," for example, is simple. As no alternatives are given with certainty we become confused and must practice patience. The *double-entendre* shows the reader that by suspending judgment he will find a new freedom from simplistic preconceptions, since, as Anderson avers, "...our ambiguous responses to language represent a complexity in our response to things." He believes that Tristram is thus trying to teach us "to recognize and make use of this fusion of the mind and the senses" (p. 972).

While Tristram desires our friendship, we tend rather to identify with him, as we see the world thorugh his eyes, and as many of our interests correspond with his.[23] Although we cannot go so far as to say that he is devious, Tristram is "guilty" of pretending to tell us one kind of story, while really giving us another. At the same time, nothing of Tristram's nature is hidden from us, so that we can "keep our distance" from him when we find him to be "unreliable." Awareness and discrimination occasioned by Tristram's instability as a narrator result in what Booth refers to as "delightful ambiguities [which] permanently enlarge our view of the possibilities of fiction" (*Rhetoric*, p. 239).

---

[22] William Bowman Piper, "Tristram Shandy's Digressive Artistry," *Studies in English Literature*, 1, No. 3 (1961), 65-76.

[23] This paragraph is based on Booth, *Rhetoric*, pp. 235-40.

As in Menippean satire, characters in *Tristram Shandy* embody mental attitudes, but each has a vital life force of his own which Tristram describes as "hobby-horsical" characterization. In *The Mental Optician* (1758), a mechanical device known as Momus's Glass is used as if it were a telescope to look into every man's heart in order to record his character.[24] Tristram criticizes this method: "Our minds shine not through the body, but are wrapt up here in a dark covering of uncrystallized flesh and blood" (I, 23). The complexity of a human character can be more adequately rendered, Tristram feels, through the device of a hobby-horse or ruling passion. That is, when a man becomes deeply attached to a favorite occupation, his character gradually takes on qualities derived from the materials belonging to that vocation. The relation between a man and his hobby-horse is in

> the manner of electrified bodies,—and that by means of the heated parts of the rider, which come immediately into contact with the back of the HOBBY-HORSE—By long journies and much friction, it so happens that the body of the rider is at length fill'd as full of HOBBY-HORSICAL matter as it can hold;—so that if you are able to give but a clear description of the nature of the one, you may form a pretty exact notion of the genius and character of the other (I, 24).

The hobby-horse is admittedly a convention, but it is more probable and intricate than a mechanical one such as the Momus's Glass.

Uncle Toby's inability to communicate leads him to his military hobby-horse. It is, in effect, an elaborate scheme which enables Toby to express without words his role in the seige of Namur, where he received a debilitating wound in the groin. In the attempt to make himself clear, he studies maps and text-books, becoming so engrossed that he builds miniature fortifications and reenacts battles with artillery made from leaden gutters, a melted-down pewter shaving-basin and the weights from sash-windows. Toby's hobby-horse, originally a therapeutic measure, becomes so intense that it spills over into other parts of the novel. Uncle Toby's minor traits are modesty, family pride and his odd mode of argument. Whenever he does not know what to say or cannot express himself in a concrete, physical way, he whistles "Lillabullero." He transmutes experience into things and

---

[24] James E. Evans, "Tristram as Critic: Momus's Glass versus Hobby-Horse," *Philological Quarterly*, 50 (1971), 669-71.

takes metaphors literally. A man of action, he identifies with generals campaigning in Europe and relives their strategies on his bowling-green. Tristram's uncle is tender-hearted, but lacks realistic knowledge of the world and of human emotions.

Walter, father of the Shandy household, represents a variation of the comic virtuoso, the "philosopher of ultimate causes."[25] Lost in speculative philosophy, he possesses knowledge, but not wisdom. While he has a deep theoretical concern for his family's welfare, he has no compassion and soon loses touch with the concrete reality of human needs and desires. "For the world of things, sensations, actions and emotions," observes McMaster, "Walter Shandy has sub-stituted a world of words, hypotheses, speculations, intellection" (p.45). He is incompetent in all things practical, and is as absurdly ineffectual as his brother Toby when it comes to real communication. "Born an orator," Walter is described almost entirely in rhetorical terminology (I, 19). He prefers getting information about people from books, relies exclusively on verbal figures for expressing emotions and regularly utters oratory rather than conversation, always talking *at* someone.[26] Walter's artificial rhetoric is supposedly a natural ten-dency, not a result of learning, and yet the "natural" orator employs the rhetorician's proofs more extensively than the conventions of classical *pronuntiatio* (rhetorical precepts on delivery) recommend. Thus does the *pater familias* parody these conditions. "Walter's frustrated attempts to portray himself by means of rhetoric form an integral part of *Tristram Shandy's* pattern," observes Graham Petrie (p. 488).

Trim is presented by Tristram as a successful rhetorician, skilled in gestures. However, the detailed presentations of Trim's postures and preparations for gesturing disclose his actual ignorance of rhet-oric. "Tristram," Farrell notes, "applauds him for just those things condemned in the *Institutes*, his 'natural' errors... given as models of artful delivery."[27] Since Tristram seems to take this all so seriously,

[25] See Stedmond, "Satire...," pp. 53-55 for examples of Walter's role in this tradition.

[26] These ideas are based on articles by Graham Petrie, "Rhetoric as Fictional Technique in *Tristram Shandy*," *Philological Quarterly*, 48 (1969), 479-94; and William J. Farrell, "Nature Versus Art as a Comic Pattern in *Tristram Shandy*," *A Journal of English Literary History*, 30 (1963), 16-35.

[27] Farrell, pp. 28-29. The *Institutes* are rhetorical texts on oration.

the comic twist must be seen as given by Sterne. In other respects, Corporal Trim is a more well-rounded and communicative person than the Shandys themselves. He is practical, resourceful and can adjust sanely to people and situations. While Toby can only describe his wound in terms of where it happened on the map of the battlefield of Namur, Trim describes it to Bridget both "geographically and anatomically" (McMaster, p. 51).

The characterization of Mrs. Shandy provides another example of Tristram's unreliability as a narrator. He presents his mother as being passive and phlegmatic, but a close reading proves otherwise. According to Ruth Marie Faurot, she can actually be considered "an early practitioner of one upmanship,"[28] clever enough to have worked out her own protective devices against Walter's argumentative nature. Several times she is actively invoved in the story: she eavesdrops in quick response to hearing "wife" in her husband's conversation, she agreeably frustrates Walter's arguments at the "beds of justice," she responds in a practical way to the sash-window accident—suggesting herbs rather than reading the history of circumcision, as does Walter—, and she shows curiosity in wanting to know "What is all this story about?" (IX, 33).

In Mary Wagoner's unusual analysis of characterization in *Tristram Shandy*, the Shandys are seen as personifications of Lockean errors.[29] In brief, there are four general types of errors: 1) The nature of ideas may be misunderstood; 2) Mistakes may occur when the mind attempts to organize the ideas it has (the false association of ideas); 3) Errors may be made in the careless and confused use and application of words; 4) Mistakes may flaw the process of judging and giving assent, because of the passions and / or other causes. Wagoner sees the hobby-horse as dramatizing "the error of wrong assent, a mind's giving way to predominant passion, inclinations" (Wagoner, p. 339), and proceeds to identify Lockean errors as key factors in the Shandean characters. While Toby is a victim of misunderstood words, Walter exemplifies the Lockean interpretation of rationalism, abusing words, using *a priori* notions, and taking delight in obscure scholastics.

---

[28] Ruth Marie Faurot, "Mrs. Shandy Observed," *Studies in English Literature*, 10 (1970), 579.

[29] Mary S. Wagoner, "Satire of the Reader in *Tristram Shandy*," *Texas Studies in Literature and Language*, 8, No. 3 (1966), 337-44.

Mrs Shandy is guilty of false associations, especially between winding the clock and "other family concernments." Yorick is witty and is thereby guilty of the hasty assemblage of ideas. Dr. Slop is enamored of his obstetrical tools (ill-equipped to judge due to a predominant passion) and submits blindly to the authority of the Catholic Church. Trim, sharing Toby's military hobby-horse, is addicted to authority and must hear military commands in order to recite his catechism. Tristam, like his father, likes to syllogize and follow scholarly pursuits to the extreme, his voice "a rational instrument for the revelation of human irrationality" (Watt, "Comic Syntax," p. 328). Even the Reader is characterized by Lockean errors in that he has problems with words, causing him to interrupt Tristram's story. "Every equivocal word," Wagoner avers, "threatens a gallop on the reader's prurient Hobby-Horse!" (p. 342). The reader has also been caught committing mental mistakes: "tis fifty to one, Sir, you are a great dunce and a blockhead" (I, 11). While lack of verbal and intellectual communication characterize the Shandean world, as exemplified by the abundance of Lockean errors, Watt holds that "sympathy and imagination" are the sources of understanding and togetherness therein.[30]

III

The Reverend Mr. Sterne (1713-1768) was not the happiest of men and did not find success until he began publishing *Tristram Shandy* at the age of forty-six. Previous to this he had been ordained and published a number of sermons and *A Political Romance* (1750). With *Tristram Shandy* he began to find himself and yet, paradoxically, he saw his life nearing an end as tuberculosis worsened his health. Like Tristram in the novel, he experienced life as a race against time and death. Sterne is most nearly identified with Tristram in Book VII in that he actually resided in Europe from 1762 to 1764, fearing death all the while. Sterne thus sought his identity and immortality through Tristram. In the process of "remembering" his early days, Tristram learns, with the perspective of age, why people acted and spoke as they did and how his past affected him. By fragmenting

---

[30] Watt, "Comic Syntax," p. 329. Watt and Wagoner, p. 343, share a similar conclusion.

himself through the analysis of his family, with which he indirectly identifies, he comes to know himself as well as he possibly can.

In 1947, at the age of eighteen, Cabrera Infante began his writing career in Havana, his world since age twelve. He wrote mostly short stories and film criticism until becoming editor for *Revolución* and *Lunes*, its literary supplement. The turning point in his life was in 1961 when his brother's film *P.M.* was censored and *Lunes* was banned. Cabrera Infante, for several years a diplomatic representative in Belgium, finally became disenchanted with the lack of intellectual and artistic freedom under the Castro regime and decided to leave Cuba permanently in 1965. In the form that *Tres Tristes Tigres* was first conceived in 1961, it is possible to correlate Cabrera Infante's purpose in writing his book with that of Sterne's. The characters of both novels comprise their own society, those in *Tres Tristes Tigres* being contemporaries of Havana night life in the 1950's. Cabrera Infante found a niche in life with his writing and sympathized with the revolutionaries against Batista. Havana was his world, a cosmos in itself. Nevertheless, after a few years with Castro it became obvious that all this was fast disappearing, and Cabrera Infante sought to preserve its essence by recording his own experiences and memories. He thus immortalized his life and his world at that particular time and place, its language, its various types and characters, its problems, concerns, joys and dreams.

Perhaps, as Holtz suggests, we can say that Cabrera Infante-Códac-Silvestre-Cué-Eribó-Bustrófedon is also a "protean creature."[31] Códac narrates "Ella cantaba boleros," which Cabrera Infante began writing in 1961 as a continuation of *P.M.*, in its celebration of Havana night life. Códac also narrates "Rompecabeza," in which we "hear" the recordings made by Bustrófedon. Códac represents Cabrera Infante as a technical and photographic recorder of the sights and sounds, people, music, language and literature of the era. Silvestre writes for *Carteles* in *Tres Tristes Tigres* with Cabrera Infante as his superior, just as Cabrera Infante had done in 1954 when a former employer became editor of *Carteles* in Havana. Silvestre's relationship with Cabrera Infante for *Carteles* suggests a similar arrangement with him for the entire novel, since he is the "author" or "compiler" of *Tres Tristes Tigres*. Silvestre also represents Cabrera Infante as a journalist

---

[31] Holtz, p. 143, in reference to Sterne and his characters.

in Havana from 1947 to 1960 in that he shares his former occupation
as well as his love for the cinema. Arsenio Cué, like the author, was
born on the twenty-second day of the month and identifies with
velocity, one of Cabrera Infante's passions as a youth. Always in
motion, always talking and always acting for a real or imagined
audience, Cué incarnates the principles of the cinema, its techniques
and its ramifications. Eribó represents Afro-Cuban rhythms, while
Bustrófedon is the essence of spoken language and the *choteo*. In sum,
each adds some quality or characteristic which might be ascribed to a
Cuban of the era portrayed by *Tres Tristes Tigres*.

Silvestre's "asides" to the reader are not as extensive as Tristram's, but they are made in the spirit of the writer who comments
on the ongoing process of literary creation. It is Coleman's opinion
that "The disruptive technique of the authorial *I* is used so that the
readers do not take the words too seriously—for is not this *I* always
the buffoon and jester?"[32] A majority of Silvestre's communications
are merely conversational or explanatory and serve to establish a
dialogue with the reader: "(por supuesto que no las voy a enumerar,
lector)" (p. 304); ".... tomé estas notas al llegar a casa)... No sé si saben,
ustedes los del otro lado de la página" (p. 344). Now and again, as
does Tristram, Silvestre will attribute a characteristic to the reader,
in this case, a lascivious nature: "La moda femenina tiende a homo...
No sean tan mal pensados. A homogeneizar..." (p. 368). By leaving
an incomplete word and sentence suspended in mid-air, the narrator
invites the reader to jump to conclusions, to participate, to write his
own version of the story. As Silvestre is the one who knows the book
already in its printed form, we assume that he is responsible for the
manner in which its parts are assembled. His control is implicit and
yet he is more sophisticated than Tristram in his direct communication with the reader.

In Cué's narration of "Casa de los espejos" we also find numerous
"asides" to the reader, all of which betray the latter's expectations for
a work of fiction. At times they are apologies: "(lo siento: no tengo
otro adjetivo... por el momento)" (p. 140). As do Eribó and Códac,
Cué wishes that the reader could see and hear whatever he is
describing, and in one instance explicitly states that he is in the

---

[32] Dorothy Gabe Coleman, *Rabelais* (London: Cambridge University
Press, 1971), p. 91.

process of writing a particular section: "de 'ala de cuervo, querido,' diría Livia por encima de mi hombro si leyera esta página mientras la escribo)" (p. 149). Many of Cué's sentences are long, run-on phrases, and at times he uses slashes rather than commas or periods. His unorthodox syntax is reminiscent of Tristram's, as are Cué's running commentaries on gestures and tone of voice which accompany his own thoughts and reactions: "Livia, levantando por primera vez su abanico ontológico y golpeando con él mi testa dura... *es malo* tono que quiere ser maternal.... Aquí hizo casi una mueca de asco" (p. 146).

IV

A comparative study also draws our attention to the narrators' preoccupation with the present moment and other Menippean qualities such as the contradictory nature of the characters, the adventure of an idea, and literary parody. A dominant feature of the narrators' characterization is their concern with time. Time-related comments in both works exemplify the oscillation between reality and fantasy or between reality and parody found in Menippean satire. Tristram's extreme interest in time is reflected in a passage in which he ponders how long it takes him to write about a given segment of his life: "at this rate I should just live 364 times faster than I should write— ...write as I will, and rush as I may into the middle of things, as Horace advises,—I shall never overtake myself—"(IV, 13). Tristram is also curious about the time it takes the reader to read, and his own sense of the passing of time. He expands and contracts time at will, always playing on the contrast between real and fictional time.[33] Silvestre's concern with time manifests itself in similar ways, when he writes: "me toma más tiempo escribirlo que lo que demoró en hacerlo" (*TTT*, p. 374). For Silvestre time has its own law of gravity (p. 306) and for Cué the cinema transforms space into time (p. 324). Silvestre's manipulation of the segments of *Tres Tristes Tigres* emphasizes the simultaneity of past, present and future. He lives in memories of the past as much as in the present, often confusing times and tenses. Laura's psychiatric sessions, which take place after all the other events, are intercalated throughout the novel. Both Tristram

---

[33] See also Mendilow, pp. 160-87.

and Silvestre seem to believe that there is only one real time " ... the present of the living being who remembers."[34]

In both characterization and general narrative technique, authors Sterne and Cabrera Infante have a proclivity for a visual or "cinematic" style of writing. Sterne, who was acquainted with painting and acting, uses gestures and vocal inflection to effect a psychological state, thereby creating a personality. If we are to believe W.B.C. Watkins, he achieves a "cinematographic effect" by describing a series of static poses in rapid succession, giving the illusion of action.[35] Cabrera Infante refers to Tres Tristes Tigres as a "gallery of voices," and we must rank him with Sterne in being skilled in pantomime, gesture and inflection of voice. In "Los debutantes" we are presented with vignettes in which the various characters are vividly described in their own words. The dialect, choice of words and tone of voice in each situation combine to suggest an image and a state of mind, creating for the reader a memorable figure. Other visual effects in both novels consist of typographical oddities such as a hand with a pointing finger, stars for left-out words, "squiggly" lines which diagram the plot line and marbled, black or blank pages in Tristram Shandy. In "Rompecabeza" of Tres Tristes Tigres there are drawings of hands and of geometrical figures, pages typed in reverse or repeating the same word throughout, blank pages and lists of names in column formation.

As is often true in the cinema, the "action" in both Tristram Shandy and Tres Tristes Tigres does not move forward in chronological progression, but rather jumps backward and forward in time with great freedom. Tristram Shandy begins in 1718 and ends in 1714, while the events in it, though centered around the years 1713-23, extend forward to 1767, and back to 1689. Sterne's method of changing time and place can be seen as cinematic, with extensive use of flashbacks, flashforwards, straight cuts and visual puns, all of which evoke Cabrera Infante's techniques. The cuts in Tristram Shandy are ususally between chapters, and lead abruptly to a new scene in medias res

---

[34] Jean-Jaques Mayoux, "Laurence Sterne" in Laurence Sterne: A Collection of Critical Essays, ed. John Traugott (Englewood Cliffs, New Jersey: Prentice-Hall, 1968), p. 120.

[35] Watson discusses this aspect of characterization in Tristram Shandy in his Perilous Balance: The Tragic Genius of Swift, Johnson, and Sterne (Princeton: Princeton University Press, 1939), pp. 131-55.

involving different characters, time and setting from those in the preceding scene or chapter.[36] Petrie cites an example of Sterne's combined use of verbal images and visual puns in maintaining continuity while moving through three distinct levels of time by means of direct cutting. In the space of just over a page and three brief chapters (VIII, 14-16) a verbal pun on "the blind gut" and the image of lighting a candle maintain the clarity while permitting shifts in time and space. In *Tres Tristes Tigres* the cuts are even more jolting, and it is often quite difficult to determine which character is speaking. Again, too, the time shifts are abrupt and more often than not give few clues as to specific time and context, at least upon a first reading. However, after discovering the keys to the book's structure, a number of temporal calculations can safely be made. For example, it seems to be a bit more than a year betwen the time Laura drops Cué—June 19, 1957 (*TTT*, p. 150)—and the announcement of Silvestre's intention to marry her (*TTT*, p. 434).[37]

The illusion of simultaneity results from these very leaps in time, space and perspective, a technique which has been cited by William Freedman as contrapuntal.[38] Tristram as narrator and Tristram's story represent two distinct but interrelated lines of simultaneous development in which thought and action are always presented as happening in the present: "I... shall lead a couple of fine lives together" (IV, 13). The culminating point of simultaneity is at Auxerre, where three levels of time, place and consciousness are juxtaposed, as it were, at the same point in time and space:

> I have been getting forwards in two different journies together, and ...I have brought myself into such a situation, as no traveller ever stood before me; for I am this moment walking

---

[36] Graham Petrie, "Note on the Novel and the Film: Flashback in *Tristram Shandy* and *The Pawnbroker*," *Western Humanities Review*, 21 (1967), 165-69. Even the smallest incident in *Tristram Shandy*, however, can be fit into its chronological order, if not dated. See the "Illustration of Sterne's use of the Time-shift," in A. A. Mendilow, *Time and the Novel* (London: P. Nevill, 1952), pp. 188-93.

[37] This assumption is also made by Juan Goytisolo, "Lectura Cervantina de *Tres Tristes Tigres*," *Revista Iberoamericana*, 42 (1976), 16.

[38] This idea is especially well-developed in William Freedman's "*Tristram Shandy*: The Art of Literary Counterpoint," *Modern Language Quarterly*, 32, No. 3 (1971), 268-80.

across the market-place of *Auxerre* with my father and my uncle *Toby*, in our way back to dinner—and I am this moment also entering *Lyons* with my postchaise broke into a thousand pieces —and I am moreover this moment in a handsome pavillion built by *Pringello*, upon the banks of the *Garonne*, which Mons. *Sligniac* has lent me, and where I now sit rhapsodizing all these affairs (VII, 28).

This sort of thing happens occasionally in *Tres Tristes Tigres*, as, for example, in "Seseribo" where two or more nights melt into one on the same street corner. However, it must be noted here that the cinematic illusion resulting from these narrative techniques of Sterne and Cabrera Infante are effected only when the reader stands back and contemplates the work in its poetic wholeness.

Menippean satire thrives on the juxtaposition of opposites, a category referred to by Bakhtin as "carnivalistic mésalliances."[39] Characterization in works of this type often reflects such "familiar-ization" of normally separate entities or values. John Traugott goes so far as to say that the characters in *Tristram Shandy*, notably Toby and Walter, are *exempla*, symbolizing conflicting attitudes.[40] A basically similar situation exists between Silvestre and Cué, whose continual contrapuntal banter is just as lacking in real communication as that of the Shandys. Some of their most engaging conversations are about "contradictorios" (TTT, pp. 407-09, 415-19). Silvestre, a writer, and Cué, a television celebrity, seem to be best of friends until their interaction receives close scrutiny. Attitudes toward remembering cause one of the essential conflicts between these comrades. Silvestre, who loves to remember, finds that memories and movies are more real to him than everyday life. Cué does not like to remember, but is an expert at quoting memorized phrases and stories. Just as charac-ters in *Tristram Shandy* always talk at cross-purposes and end up frustrating themselves and others, the specific perspective of each of the Havana night creatures holds its own significant memories and associations, which also results in poor communication. In both, many truths are spoken in jest or in punning language. When the real truth is spoken in a straightforward way, it is either purposely

---

[39] Mikhail Bakhtin, *Dostoevsky's Poetics* (Ann Arbor: Ardis, 1973), p. 101.

[40] *Tristram Shandy's World: Sterne's Philosophical Rhetoric* (Berkeley: University of California Press, 1954).

not heard, or it causes the end of the relationship, as with the Widow Wadman and Toby, and with Cué and Silvestre. What holds the Shandys together is their mutual good-will and family ties. The tigers share the scintillating Havana night life of the fifties.

The main characters in both *Tristram Shandy* and *Tres Tristes Tigres* at times parody or caricature their particular profession, "type" or social class. In *Tristram Shandy*, Walter is the verbal virtuoso and Tristram, the scatterbrained writer, while Toby rides his military hobby-horse. In *Tres Tristes Tigres*, Bustrófedon is the phantom of the spoken word, Códac, the photo-journalist, La Estrella, the black singer, monster of the night, Eribó, the mulatto bongo player, Vivian Smith-Corona, the rich young *criolla*, and so on. But most of the characters are actually rounded in the overall context in that we see them develop, some more than others, as they show themselves in different aspects to various people. Howard Anderson believes that Sterne uses his characters to comment upon assumptions and actions of particular social classes.[41] Toby, for example, as an aristocratic warrior, is a parody of the upper classes. The "good master" Toby has his "good servant" Corporal Trim, who respects Toby so much that he followed his wounded leader home to continue to serve him. Toby and Trim are now dependent upon each other for more than money and work. *Tres Tristes Tigres*, on the other hand, exposes social classes and racial and national differences as determining status and mobility. Eribó cannot advance as a commercial artist due to his color. He is also socially inferior to Vivian, who can tell him her secret but cannot get involved with him. The U.S. foreigner is parodied more than most in the stories written by Mr. Campbell.

Women play a relatively minor role in both novels. Mrs. Shandy is thought by Tristram to be passive, phlegmatic and implicitly guilty of the dubious beginnings he had. Women are seen as inferior by Walter Shandy; he brushes the midwife aside in favor of Dr. Slop, who then proceeds to ruin Tristram's nose with his forceps. The Widow Wadman is lustful, but extremely cautious, her love for Toby seen as an attack on his modesty. Women in *Tres Tristes Tigres* are for the most part sexual temptresses who excel in good looks and come-ons, except for La Estrella, respected for her voice, and Laura, for her integrity.

[41] "A Version of Pastoral: Class and Society in *Tristram Shandy*," *Studies in English Literature*, 7 (1967), 509-29.

Several themes common to both *Tristram Shandy* and *Tres Tristes Tigres* touch on some of the basic enigmas of life, such as death, sex and the problem of identity, often providing instances of ideas as adventures. The same problems are faced by Sterne and Tristram: "the imminence of death, the running out of time, the dissolution of identity" (Holtz, p. 134). The prominent theme of death in *Tristram Shandy* prefigures Sterne's own death: Yorick's death is punctuated with a black page (I), Bobby's death startles the household (V), Le Fever's death provides the acme of sentimental situations for Toby (VI), and Tristram's flight from death occupies all of Volume VII. In this version of the "Dance of Death," Tristram scurries across France, fearing he will not have enough time to finish writing his *Life and Opinions*.

The strategy from *One Thousand and One Nights*, of not finishing a story as a ruse for staying alive, is employed in *Tristram Shandy* and in *Tres Tristes Tigres*. Trim is repeatedly frustrated in his efforts to tell the story of the King of Bohemia, and Toby insists on not giving specific dates (VIII, 19). In "Bachata" Cué and Silvestre try to tell the story of Silvestre being left nude in the park, but, like the song of "Tres Palabras," it never begins.

Death is present on two levels in *Tres Tristes Tigres*: the personal or experiential and the symbolic. As a child, Silvestre sees a man fatally shot. Cué believes that he has been shot when a black page terminates that section of "Los debutantes." Laura's shock upon seeing a cadaver in her boyfriend's bathtub can be related to Cabrera Infante's youth, when he became discouraged about continuing medical school by the gruesome task of dissecting human corpses. Bustrófedon relates the seven versions of the death of Trotsky. A literary parody, true, but it also deals with one of the original leaders of the Russian Revolution, whose death was a legend in the Latin American consciousness. Cabrera Infante could also be making a caricature of Castro's regime as it affects literary freedom. It may well be that the death of artistic freedom in Cuba is being revealed in this section, which suggests that Cuban writers must now express themselves on approved topics only. Bustrófedon's death represents the demise of freedom of expression, and of the vibrant and alive *choteo* of the happy Cuba of yore. Laura's dream foretells the death and destruction of pre-Castro Cuba.

"How can there be an enduring identity in a world of ceaseless change?" queries Holtz. "*Tristam Shandy* can be seen, I think, as an expression of this dilemma and as an implied answer to it" (p. 134). Sterne was in a sense creating an identity as he created *Tristram Shandy*, a work which Stedmond cites as "an early example of the dynamic organicism often associated with Romanticism" ("Genre...," p. 48). The comic mode of *Tristram Shandy*, with its emphasis on fixed and fixated characters and its lack of emphasis on chronological time, is congenial to a sense of continuity. Tristram's book "*is* his self in a symbolic transformation" (Holtz, p. 138), wherein Sterne-Tristram as "artist-hero" seeks to immortalize his identity. But Holtz affirms that Sterne is aware of his limitations as well, since he illustrates "the limited control of art over life, the impossibility of a total reconstruction of one's identity, the conditional nature of the artist's immortality" (p. 148). Due to his awareness of the theories of Locke and Hume, which seem to lead to a denial of personal identity, Sterne is constantly concerned with the problem of "the fragmentation of the self" ("Genre...," p. 48), a preoccupation of many twentieth century novelists: "—My good friend, quoth I—as sure as I am I—and you are you—And who are you? said he—Don't puzzle me; said I" (VIII, 33).

Each of the characters in *Tres Tristes Tigres* is presented in a fragmented manner due to the apparently erratic constuction of the novel. Nonetheless, continuity is provided in both works by the relatively "fixed" characters, and by the atemporal, comic mode of the work. We do see changes in Cué and Silvestre, who are especially preoccupied about their vocations as writers. Cué asks: "—¡Qué sería yo entonces? ¿Un lector mediocre más? ¿Traductor, otro traidor?" (p. 340). The problem of identity is perhaps most obvious in the character of the "unknown" female who is undergoing psychoanalysis. She is actively trying to find herself by recreating scenes from her past and by analyzing her dreams. The identity of Magalena, who appears sporadically throughout *Tres Tristes Tigres*, is a puzzle to Cué and Silvestre. Djelal Kadir, who treats *Tres Tristes Tigres* as a pop art object, touches on the problem of identity: "In the spinning complexity of verbal games, in the category of contraries and the string of contradictions elaborated by Silvestre,...self-denial and self-affirmation become analogous. In the antics of the actor Cué, the acquisition of an identity is equivalent to the loss of identity."[42] Most important is the

[42] Djelal Kadir, "Pop Art and the New Spanish American Novel," *Journal of Spanish Studies; Twentieth Century*, 2 (1974), 133.

subtle development of Silvestre's sense of self, which finally leads to the rejection of his former life and friends.

If sexual themes are symbolic, then *Tristram Shandy* can be interpreted as a comedy of emotional and intellectual impotence,[43] and *Tres Tristes Tigres* as one of emotional and intellectual frustration. Sex is a central symbol in *Tristram Shandy*, which "begins with a joke about begetting and ends with a joke about impotence."[44] The sexual topics broached in the first chapters are sexual intercourse, gestation periods, fertility, sterility and birth, all of which are paralleled in Volume IX with reference to Obadiah and the Shandy Bull. As Booth notes, all the Shandy males, including the bull, seem to be plagued with implications of impotence. This is seen in Tristram's failures with Jenny and Nannette and his childlessness, Toby's sterile amours with the Widow Wadman and Walter's poor performance on delivery of the *homunculus*.[45] Sexual relations and implications are prevalent in *Tres Tristes Tigres*, but the theme tends more towards frustration and lack of fulfillment than impotence. Examples are Aurelita's voyeurism and insinuated sexual play under the truck as a child, Eribó's failure with Vivian and Cué's with Laura, Códac's "romantic" encounters with La Estrella, Irenita and Cuba Venegas, and the loose ways of Livia and Magalena.

Once again the presence of literary parody in the two works in question underscores the attitude of caricature and burlesque at the heart of Menippean satire. In addition to Sterne's pointing out a number of shortcomings in the traditional novel and demonstrating preferable techniques, he is believed by some to be making a parody of the sentimental novel, popular in the first half of the seventeenth century. Melvyn New holds that "The persistent reduction of human love to its physical manifestations is the weapon Sterne brings to

---

[43] A. R. Towers in "Sterne's Cock and Bull Story," *A Journal of English Literary History*, 24 (1957), 12-29, posits that the theme of sex is an integral part of character creation and a vehicle for other themes in *Tristram Shandy*. With regard to characterization he discusses the following topics: Tristram and the comedy of inadequacy, Uncle Toby and the comedy of displacement, Walter Shandy and the comedy of frustration.

[44] Elizabeth Drew, *A Modern Guide to Fifteen English Masterpieces* (New York: W. W. Norton, 1963), p. 77.

[45] Wayne C. Booth, "Did Sterne Complete *Tristram Shandy?*" *Modern Philology*, 48 (1951), 182.

bear against the sentimental view of man which Toby embodies."[46] Tristram's uncle, who literally "wouldn't hurt a fly," nevertheless revels in mock battles, oblivious to the reality of war as an instrument of death and destruction. Likewise, his amours are a futile imitation of an intimate relationship. Toby's humanitarianism is hypocritical and represents Sterne's "satiric evaluation of the sentimental vision."

Besides Bustrófedon's literary parodies, Cabrera Infante's book also includes parodies of poets like Rubén Darío and José Martí, and of translators in general. The section entitled "Los Visitantes" is expressly devoted to such a parody. The second version of "Historia de un bastón" (pp. 185-203) is described in Cabrera Infante's note to Silvestre (p. 439) as a poor Spanish translation by Rine of Mr. Campbell's story, originally written in English. The first version (pp. 173-84) is Silvestre's work, in which he presumably improved upon Rine's translation by merely placing the adjectives after the nouns instead of before them. By revealing the foibles of translators, especially if unqualified, the narrator provides us with an excellent example of *Tristramshandyism*. We are made aware of the techniques of writing, almost to the exclusion of understanding their relevancy to the text.

IV

Northrup Frye refers to *Tristram Shandy* as a mixture of Menippean satire and novel. I contend that precisely in this way *Tres Tristes Tigres* can be meaningfully analyzed, rather than as a disorganized novel. It is characteristic of Menippean satire to be fragmented and essentially plotless. While in *Tristram Shandy* the narrator claims he has two stories to tell us, his childhood and his "sentimental" relationship with the Widow Wadman, the latter story is used to keep the reader in suspense until the end of nine volumes. Just as Tristram's intentional digressions break up the forward-moving action of the plot, so too the narrators of *Tres Tristes Tigres* confuse the reader. Looking back on the work one finds that a sketchy love triangle keeps the reader in suspense until the outcome is revealed at the very end of the book.

---

[46] This paragraph summarizes Melvyn New, *Laurence Sterne as Satirist* (Gainesville: University of Florida Press, 1969), pp. 195-200. Quotes from pp. 195, 200.

From the hobby-horsical to "contradictorios," characters in both works represent conflicting or contrasting attitudes. In general, both works attribute more importance to opinions, ideas and cultural knowledge than to the story line. Erudite enunciations or listings in *Tristram Shandy* are, for example, the sermon (II, 17), a list of arguments used in formal logic (I, 21), the memorandum to the Doctors of the Sorbonne in French (I, 20) and Slawkenbergius' Tale presented in parallel texts in Latin and English (IV). In *Tres Tristes Tigres* "Los pro-y-contra nombres" provides for a cataloguing of famous people in a parodic vein. Indeed, the comic element pervades all levels of these works, as characters of all types are mocked. While in *Tres Tristes Tigres* translators, writers and pedants are the targets, in *Tristram Shandy* it is the philosopher and the orator. Walter Shandy is the intellectual incapable of relating his knowledge to human problems, and Trim is an orator who breaks all the rules of rhetoric.

An abbreviated form of Menippean satire is the intellectual debate or symposium in which a conflict of ideas supercedes interest in personalities. One of many such dialogues in *Tristram Shandy* takes place after dinner around the table, when the misnaming of Tristram is discussed. The narrator makes a burlesque of the serious occasion by giving as much importance to the hot chestnut which lands in Phutatorius' lap as he gives the learned topic. Similarly, in the "Bachata" sections of *Tres Tristes Tigres*, which comprise one-third of the book, conversational banter by far outweighs action. The seriousness of the interchange between Silvestre and Cué is undermined by the narrator's continuous exposure of insincerity and lack of real communication.

It is appropriate at this point to cite Silvestre's lines which pay homage to Tristram, as he seems to be referring expressly to one of two possible scenes in *Tristram Shandy*. In one, it takes five chapters for Walter Shandy to get down a flight of stairs (IV, 9-13). In the other, Uncle Toby is left knocking the ashes out of his pipe, forgotten until many chapters later (I, 21). Silvestre writes:

> Me detuve. ¿Ustedes conocen ese acto en que de veras uno se detiene en una conversación, sin hablar caminando, que la palabra y el gesto se detienen al mismo tiempo, que la voz se calla y la gesticulación se inmoviliza? (p. 420).

The books of Sterne and Cabrera Infante offer us an unusual experi-

ence, that of participating in a humorous rendition of literary creativity. The narrators of *Tres Tristes Tigres* capture the essence of
Tristramshandyism, but carry it far beyond the level divulged by Tristram. While the latter lays bare to the reader his narrative techniques, *Tres Tristes Tigres* is a challenge directed to the reader by
Cabrera Infante to piece together the puzzle proposed by the work.

⚜ 3 ⚜

A Study in Betrayal:
Tres Tristes Tigres

RES TRISTES TIGRES exposes and sheds light on a universal human problem: language, in its many forms, as betrayal. His concern with this predicament provides the underlying unity pervading the theme, the form and the very medium of *Tres Tristes Tigres*. In his own "Epilogue for Late(nt) Readers," Cabrera Infante states that the theme of *Tres Tristes Tigres* is "three-fold treason (in language, in literature and in love.)"[1] The author, the character-narrators and the reader are throughout involved in a chain reaction of betrayals which make up the fabric of the novel and which are comments on communication and literature outside the novel as well as within it.

This molding of an entire work around a single idea is recognized as a central feature of Menippean works:

> The most important characteristic of the menippea lies in the fact that the most daring and unfettered fantasies (*Fantastika*) and adventures are internally motivated, justified and illumi-

[1] Guillermo Cabrera Infante, "Epilogue for Late(nt) Readers," *Review '72* (1971-72), p. 28 .

nated here by a purely ideological and philosophical end—to create *extraordinary situations* in which to provoke and test a philosophical idea—the word, or the *truth*.... not the testing of a specific individual or social-typical human character.... the content of the menippea consists of the adventures of an *idea* or the *truth* in the world.[2]

Bakhtin goes on to emphasize that Menippean satire is a genre of "ultimate questions," in which non-academic philosophical problems "with an ethico-practical inclination... are put to the test" (p. 95).

If we were to abstract from *Tres Tristes Tigres* a philosophical idea of the sort referred to by Bakhtin, we would deduce that Cabrera Infante deals with problems relevant to communication caused by the imperfect nature of language and man's tendency to be a deceiver. We might find that, in effect, *Tres Tristes Tigres* explores questions such as: Can man overcome his natural instinct for betrayal? Is there any hope for love in the world, given the difficulties involved in communication? Is it possible to express the truth through language?

The following three-part analysis will demonstrate the manifestation of betrayal on all levels of *Tres Tristes Tigres*, and in countless guises. The form of *Tres Tristes Tigres* is that of a literary composition which finds its origin and structure in music, and its language and characterization in rhythm and sound. A thematic analysis of character interaction centers on love, with a host of variations, from narcissism to doppelgängers and love triangles. The inescapable medium is language, the central enigma of *Tres Tristes Tigres* as personified by Bustrófedon and as used by the various character-narrators in an attempt to express the elusive reality they share.

I

Cabrera Infante began writing *Tres Tristes Tigres* in 1961 as a reaction to two events which profoundly affected him: first, the censure and confiscation of his brother's film *P. M.*, the theme of which was Havana night life in the 1950's, and, secondly, the sudden death of Fredy, a popular Cuban vocalist, in Puerto Rico:

---

[2] Mikhail Bakhtin, *Problems of Dostoevsky's Poetics*, trans. R. W. Rotsel (Ann Arbor: Ardis, 1973), p. 94.

Es cierto que mi intención era recobrar La Habana y al mismo tiempo continuar *P. M.* por otros medios, tal vez menos idóneos, al tiempo que celebraba la vida y la muerte de La Estrella, ya no más Fredy pero un personaje literario. Era inevitable que la música fuera el fondo del libro pero como la forma, es decir la superficie, es para mí más profunda que el tema, invariablemente formas musicales cubanas dictaron la estructura del libro.[3]

Cabrera Infante's statement that the form is more profound than the theme would seem to imply that he feels that the form carries at least as much meaning as the content. This belies an aspiration to produce an artistic work with a quality inherent in music: the fusion or identity of form and content. The theme of *Tres Tristes Tigres is* the structure and rhythm of the work, perhaps as much as is possible in a literary creation. The author does not choose to verbalize a message, but rather offers us the experience of his book as a *gestalt.* "Because the forms of human feeling are much more congruent with musical forms than with the forms of language," declares Susanne K. Langer, "music can *reveal* the nature of feelings with a detail and truth that language cannot approach.... Not communication but insight is the gift of music...."[4]

A. A. Mendilow suggests that the modern novel, in trying to create a new reality for itself, experiments with techniques from other media such as music in an attempt to bypass the limitations inherent in the symbolic medium upon which literature is entirely dependent, language. "The closed plot has given pride of place to wider rhythms which often tend to approximate to the movements of music."[5] It should not be a surprise, then, to learn that Cabrera Infante finds that the form of *Tres Tristes Tigres* resembles that of the rhapsody: "Al final, cuando el libro estuvo terminado, me encontré con que su forma se semejaba mucho a la rapsodia" (30 September 1978). Our interest in the rhapsody is two-fold. On the one hand, a

---

[3] Letter to author from Cabrera Infante, 30 September 1978. Further quotations from letters will be identified only with their dates.

[4] Susanne K. Langer, *Philosophy in a New Key* (Cambridge: Harvard University Press, 1971), 3rd ed., pp. 235, 244.

[5] A. A. Mendilow, *Time and the Novel* (New York: Humanities Press, 1972), p. 38.

rhapsody is a musical composition for instruments which is irregular in form and resembles an improvisation. The etymological roots of "rhapsody" also pertain to the parallels which can be drawn with *Tres Tristes Tigres*, since the Greek rhapsodist was a professional reciter or chanter of epic poetry, a genre often considered to be the forerunner of the novel. Eric Blom avers that "The rhapsody was the song of the *rhapsode*; a sequel of rhapsodies when sung in succession or written down so as to form a series, constituted an epic poem, and when a long poem was chanted in sections at different times and by different singers it was said to be "rhapsodized."[6]

At a glance, we can see obvious reasons for the musical analogy between *Tres Tristes Tigres* and the rhapsody. Cabrera Infante's novel is divided into sections "spoken" by different characters or narrators. In his "Advertencia" we read:

> El libro está en cubano. Es decir, escrito en los diferentes dialectos del español que se hablan en Cuba y la escritura no es más que un intento de atrapar la voz humana al vuelo, como aquel que dice ... algunas páginas se deben oír mejor que se leen, y no sería mala idea leerlas en voz alta (p. 9).

Thus, as in epic poetry where the sections were chanted or sung, *Tres Tristes Tigres* is a "rhapsodized" work. Also applicable to both is the tendency towards improvisation. Musicians may speak of a rhapsody of tunes as "A string of melodies arranged with a view to effective performance in public, but without regular dependence of one part upon another" (Blom, p. 145). The independence of the various parts of a rhapsody also occurs in *Tres Tristes Tigres*, for the book is introduced in its "Prólogo" by the Master of Ceremonies as a performance to be presented "without words but with music and happiness and joy...." Its numerous divisions are, as acts in a show, relatively independent. "Ever since Liszt's *Hungarian Rhapsodies* there has been a tendency among composers to associate the term "rhapsody" with music of a national (or folkloric) character" (Blom, p. 145).

While these characteristics associated with the rhapsody are not essential to the genre, they are present in an implicit way in *Tres Tristes Tigres*, written for and about the people in a specific location in

---

[6] Eric Blom, ed., *Grove's Dictionary of Music and Musicians* (New York: St. Martin's Press, 1955), 5th ed., vol. VII, p. 144.

Cuba. Furthermore, the title and several sections of the book are derived from folklore. Nevertheless, the affinity which Cabrera Infante finds between *Tres Tristes Tigres* and the rhapsody is not with the popular *Hungarian Rhapsodies*, but rather, the rhapsody as exemplified by the symphonic work of Bela Bartok, *Concerto for Orchestra* (1943).

> Estaba habituado, por mi educación musical, a despreciar la rapsodia, ejemplificada en las Rapsodias Húngaras de Lizst, que sonaban a música barata. Pero me di cuenta de que una de la obras maestras de la música del primer medio siglo XX, el *Concerto for Orchestra*, de nada menos que Bela Bartok—¡era una rapsodia! Si esta forma musical había sido tomada prestada por la música a la literatura, bien podría aprovechar y acogerme en su refugio. Pero en realidad la pieza de Bartok estaba lejos de mi mente no ya cuando empecé a escribir *Tres Tristes Tigres* sino cuando ya lo había terminado (30 September 1978).

Although Cabrera Infante was not directly influenced by Bartok's work, as he was by various literary predecessors, it is still suitable to consider briefly this work to which Cabrera Infante refers as a rhapsody. The *Concerto for Orchestra* is in essence a symphony in that it is a cyclical instrumental composition for a full orchestra. However, its five movements (in contrast to the symphony's four) do not correspond closely to the usual progression of sonata, lyrical, minuet and trio, rondo or sonata form. Its title relates it to the eighteenth century *concerto grosso* in which groups of solo instruments are contrasted with the full body of the orchestra.

Both Bartok's *Concerto* and *Tres Tristes Tigres* are cyclical compositions in that the final section harks back to the first, through its form or an allusion. The closing words of Silvestre in "Bachata" refer to "la clave del alba," Aurelita, the little girl in the first section of "Los debutantes" at the beginning of the book. The "Epílogo" consists of the babbling of a crazy woman, whose meaningless chatter reflects her lack of a sense of time and reality, which suggests circularity as she forever repeats herself. The solo instruments would be the main narrators of *Tres Tristes Tigres* as against the peripheral characters representing the orchestration of Havana night life. The sections of the book do not follow regular chapters as in the traditional novel, but they are indexed and titled, as are the movements of the *Concerto*. The divisions of *Tres Tristes Tigres* may be likened to their musical counterparts as follows:

"Prólogo": Introit, in which the Master of Ceremonies explicitly announces a musical show:

> Sin palabras pero con música y sana alegría y esparcimiento...
> Without words but with music and happiness and joy...¡Para ustedes!...To you all! Nuestro primer gran show de la noche...¡en Tropicana! Our first great show of the evening...In Tropicana! ¡Arriba el telón!...Curtains up! (p. 19).

"Los debutantes": Overture, in which musical themes are introduced. The seven brief sketches introduce characters as motifs or melodies whose interactions in the remainder of the work produce harmony, dissonance or counterpoint. These occurrences will include repetitions of, and variations on, the original motifs.

"Seseribo": Solo of Afro-Cuban rhythms played on the bongo.

"La casa de los espejos": Solo by Cué. Part I has a rapid tempo which characterizes Cué's constant movement and desire for activity for its own sake. Part II is a rare instance of reverie and nostalgia for Cué, with a slower tempo.

"Los visitantes": Theme and variation, two versions of the same story or piece, one played well, the other played in an extremely clumsy manner. The player (translator) of the variation lacks a knowledge of the medium in which he is working.

"Rompecabeza": A multi-media movement for waking up the audience, it actually includes the following two sections.

"La muerte de Trotsky referida por varios escritores cubanos, años después—o antes": Seven variations on a theme.

"Algunas revelaciones": A rest with a hold, silence being an integral part of music.

"Bachata": Fugue and counterpoint, in which two or more melodies are combined to give a satisfying musical texture and produce good harmony by the interaction of parts. The internal rhythms of main characters Silvestre and Cué are such that there is a constant tension between them. Musicologist von Hoeslin makes a similar analogy:

> The fundamental relationships in music, he says, are *tensions and resolutions;* and the patterns generated by these functions are the patterns exemplified in all art, and also in all emotive responses. Wherever sheer contrasts of ideas produce a reaction, wherever experiences of pure form produce mental tension, we have the essence of *melody*...(Langer, p. 227).

Silvestre, as narrator of "Bachata," tries to establish whenever possible a *largo* movement, with his reflections and memories. His tempo is a slow *ritardando*, his volume *diminuendo*, as his thoughts are silent more often than spoken. The counterpoint of Cué's fast tempo, *accelerando* with the *staccatto* of quotes and definitive statements, interrupts and balances Silvestre's slower tempo. Their contrasting attitudes towards time and memory often produce rapid, spontaneous discussions, jokes and plays on words which create a harmony in *presto* tempo.

A somewhat analogous contrapuntal harmony is seen in the juxtaposition of the stories of the two main female characters of *Tres Tristes Tigres*. "Ella cantaba boleros" and the psychiatric sessions of Laura Díaz appear alternately throughout the book (as can be seen on the chart, p. 59). Although both are represented in numerous isolated sections, each has a sustained theme. La Estrella's story may be likened to the ground bass, and the "Sessions" to an embellishment motif, as these sections are usually much shorter than the "Ella cantaba boleros" sections. Once again, the internal rhythms of these two characters are diametrically opposed. La Estrella is a creature of the night, Laura of the day. One is physically monstrous, the other slender and beautiful. Although one knows her talent and will let no one sway her, the other allows Livia to teach her how to walk, talk and dress, converting her into "un cisne de Avon Inc" (p. 149). Finally, La Estrella knows herself and her destiny, while Laura goes to the psychiatrist at her husband's request and admits she is uncertain of her own identity.

"Epílogo": Coda, or final passage of a musical composition, which gives it a satisfactory ending. In *Tres Tristes Tigres*, the crazy lady babbling in the park can take no more.

In its adjectival sense, a rhapsody is an utterance or writing marked by extravagant enthusiasm. *Tres Tristes Tigres* and many of its characters can be described in this way:

> Con todo considero que más que un bolero o una canción *feeling* mi libro parece una rapsodia, inclusive en términos retóricos es rapsódico, sobre todo cuando quiere ser musical, cuando exalta la visión y la audición de La Estrella, cuando canta a su vida que sólo se realiza en la canción (30 September 1978).

The story of La Estrella is narrated by the photo-journalist Códac in the eight sections entitled "Ella cantaba boleros." His job took him to

EXPANDED INDEX

The indented entries are additions to the "Índice" of *Tres Tristes Tigres*, facilitating the location of the eight sections of "Ella cantaba boleros" and the eleven psychiatric sessions.

the night clubs, where he met La Estrella one night during a *chowcito*, a meeting of night people who sing and dance from after the last show until dawn:

> Pues allá en el centro del chowcito estaba ahora la gorda vestida con un vestido barato, de una tela carmelita cobarde que se confundía con el chocolate de su piel chocolate y unas sandalias viejas, malucas, y un vaso en la mano, moviéndose al compás de la música, moviendo las caderas, todo su cuerpo de una manera bella, no obscena pero sí sexual y bellamente, meneándose a ritmo, canturreando por entre los labios aporreados, sus labios gordos y morados, a ritmo, agitando el vaso a ritmo, rítmicamente, bellamente, artísticamente ahora y el efecto total era de una belleza tan distinta, tan horrible, tan nueva que lamenté no haber llevado la cámara para haber retratado aquel elefante que bailaba ballet, aquel hipopótamo en punta, aquel edificio movido por la música y le dije a Irenita, antes de preguntarle el nombre, interrumpiéndome cuando preguntaba el nombre, al preguntarle el nombre, Es la salvaje belleza de la vida, sin que me oyera naturalmente, sin que me entendiera si me había oído, naturalmente y le dije, le pregunté, le dije Quién es, tú. Ella me dijo con un tono muy desagradable, Es la caguama que canta, la única tortuga que canta boleros, y se río...(p. 64).

La Estrella always sings without accompaniment: "a ella le sobra la música" (p. 68). When Códac meets her, she is living in the house of the well-known radio figure Alex Bayer as an uninvited guest. Alex considers her a cosmic phenomenon and says that she "canta cuando regresa por la mañana, canta en la ducha, canta arreglándose para salir y siempre canta" (p. 83). La Estrella is obsessed with becoming a famous singer and has a fear of dying before achieving her goal. Códac wants to help her, so he holds a party in her honor to which she does not come until he lures her to his apartment under false pretenses. La Estrella does gain some fame, but she dies an untimely death in Mexico. Códac's mortal hatred for forgetting drives him to write La Estrella's story, so that people will remember her and her style of singing. "La Estrella era el Lutero de la música cubana y siempre estuvo en lo firme, como si ella que no sabía leer ni escribir tuviera en la música sus sagradas escrituras pautadas" (p. 281).

Gloria Pérez' success story supplies a strong contrast to La Estrella's, whose singing is raw, natural and exquisitely beautiful. Gloria Pérez sells out for fame as Cuba Venegas, and sings "civilized" music, always with accompaniment. Códac says it is much better to see Cuba than to hear her. Eribó hears Cuba's voice coming up from the garbage cans in the street while she is singing in the Mil Novecientos, a nightclub in the basement of the building, suggesting that her music is "canned" and of the worst kind.

Like La Estrella, Eribó has "soul," personifies Afro-Cuban rhythms and may represent Cabrera Infante's love for music and the fulfillment of a childhood fantasy to play the bongo.[7] Eribó, "el St. Exupéry del son," narrates the Seseribo section of *Tres Tristes Tigres* and at times describes his experience of playing the bongo as if he were flying. He captures a light and airy sensation by repeating the gerund *tocando* with onomatopoeic and rhythmic results:

> Seguía *tocando* y *tocando* vi a Arsenio Cué llamar al camarero y pedir la cuenta *tocando* y *tocando* despertar a Silvestre y vi al prieto escritor levantarse y empezar a salir con Vivian y Sibila cogidas de los brazos y *tocando* Cué estaba pagando él solo bastante y *tocando* regresó el camarero y Cué le dio una propina *tocando* que pareció buena por la cara del camarero satisfecho *tocando* y lo vi irse a él también y reunirse todos en la puerta y el botones abrir las cortinas y *tocando* salieron por la sala de juego roja y verde y bien alumbrada y la cortina cayó sobre, detras de ellos *tocando*. No me dijeron ni hasta luego. Pero no me importó porque estaba *tocando* y seguía *tocando* y todavía iba a seguir *tocando* un buen rato (p. 99) (emphasis added).

Another selection from "Seseribo" shows a similar use of the gerund with a number of different verbs:

> ...y yo allí *picando, repicando, tumbando, haciendo* contracanto, *llevando* con el pie el compás, *midiendo* mentalmente el ritmo, *vigilando* esa clave interior que todavía suena... *contando* el silencio mi silencio, mientras oigo el sonido de la orquesta, *haciendo* piruetas, clavados, giros, rizos con el tambor de la izquierda, luego con el de la derecha, con los dos, *imitando* un accidente, una picada, *engañando* al del cencerro o al trompeta o al bajo, *atravesándome* sin decir que es un contratiempo, *haciendo* como que me atravieso, *regresando* al tiempo, *cuadrando, enderezando* el aparato y por último *aterrizando*: *jugando* con la música *tocando sacando* música de aquel cuero de chivo doble clavado a un dado a un cubo de madera

---

[7] Rita Guibert, *Seven Voices* (New York: Knopf, 1973), p. 429.

chivo inmortalizado su berrido hecho música entre las piernas como los testículos de la música *yendo* con la orquesta *estando* con ella y sin embargo tan fuera de la soledad y de la compañía y del mundo: en la música. *Volando* (p. 112) (emphasis added).

Besides these two characters which represent Afro-Cuban music and rhythms, and their antithesis Cuba Venegas, there are many other musical elements to be found in *Tres Tristes Tigres*, including a great love for music on the part of the other main characters: Códac, Silvestre (writer), Arsenio Cué (actor), Rine Leal (critic) and Bustrófedon (anagrammatist and "writer" of oral literature). The characters live in a frenzy of movement, with music providing a focus or unity to their existence. When certain of these characters get together, it is as if they were engaged in a musical conference. There is always music in the background, whether it is a record, a live singer or the radio. When the friends are having a "recording" session, they record, among other things, popular songs and tangos sung by Rine and bongo rhythms played by Eribó on the table. Several times the narrator says "había que oírlo" or "hay que oírlo." There are innumerable lines from popular Cuban songs mixed in with dialogue and the book's narration. At times they are parodies of those songs. The characters are always naming singers, composers, musicians and groups of musicians, both Cuban and foreign, and when drunk they make wordplays on the names of famous scores and composers.

Eribó is so completely immersed in music that when he hears women talk, he often imagines that certain phrases would be appropriate titles for a *bolero*. Such is the case when Cuba says "Aprende a perdonarme" (p. 113), and Vivian says "La vida es terrible" (p. 116). On many occasions the narrators speak of their activities in musical terminology, at times using neologisms, as in Bustrófedon's "(Afinando su guitarronca voz)" (p. 210). Silvestre describes Cué's movements as he is driving:

> Cué manejaba y al mismo tiempo *tarareaba la música* con la cabeza y con las manos avanzando un *forte* con el puño cerrado y siguiendo un *pianissimo* con la mano abierta y hacia abajo, bajando *una escalera musical* invisible, imaginaria, y parecía un maestro de sordomudos traduciendo un discurso (p. 295) (emphasis added).

Cué's pastime of complaining about everything under the sun is referred to as "su tema musical" (p. 100). Livia shouts a message to

Silvestre and Cué "en soprano callejera" (p. 143). When the tigers make wordplays on each other's names, Códac says: "Nos pusimos a cantar todas las variantes de todos los nombres de la gente que conocemos, que es juego secreto..." (p. 211). One of the best examples of this ritual is the list of variations on Rine Leal's name:

> Bustrofedonte (que era el nombre esa semana para Rine, a quien llamaba no solamente el más leal amigo del hombre, sino Rineceronte, Rinedocente, Rinedecente, Rinecente, como luego hubo un Rinecimiento seguido del Rinesimiento, Rinesimento, Rinefermento, Rinefermoso, Rineferonte, Rinoferante, Bonoferviente, Buonofarniente, Busnofedante, Bustodedante, Bustofedonte: variantes que marcaban las variaciones de la amistad: palabras como un termómetro) (p. 207).

Amongst Rine's imaginary inventions is the machine which types musical notes. Silvestre and Cué describe it in amusing detail:

> —Es una invención tan revolucionaria que ya ha sido prohibida, oficialmente, en todos los conservatorios. Hay un acuerdo firmado en Ginebra para impedir su uso. Igual destino tuvo su sexofón sucedáneo del violónceloso.... Papapapááá papapapí sería el comienzo, por ejemplo, de la Quinta Sinfonía de Beethoven, que Rine tiene ya casi toda transcrita a su sistema. El solfeo, por supuesto, se llamará tarareo. Ya lo verán, Rine resultará más importante en la historia de la música que Czerny (p. 385).

A page entitled "Partitura" is completely covered with the repetition of the meaningless word *Blen* (p. 322), included in *Tres Tristes Tigres* as a tribute to Chano Pozo's *guaracha*, an example of pure musical *choteo*.

A typical conversation between Silvestre and Cué as they are driving around Havana listening to classical music on the radio is the following:

> —Entonces, ¿qué te parece Vivaldi a sesenta?
> —Que bajaste la velocidad.
> —Albinoni a ochenta, Frescobaldi a cien, Cimarosa a cincuenta, Monteverdi a cientoveinte, Gesualdo a lo que dé el motor—hizo una pausa más exaltada que refrescante y siguió:—No importa, lo que yo dije sigue valiendo y pienso en lo que será Palestrina oído en un jet.
> —Un milagro de la acústica—dije yo (p. 298).

They believe they are hearing Bach and make word plays with his name:

> ...y pensé en los juegos verbales que hubiera hecho Bustró-
> fedon de estar vivo: Bach, Bachata, Bachanal, Baches (que había
> en el pavimento, rompiendo el continuo espacial del Malecón),
> Bachillerato, Bacharat, Bacaciones—y oírlo hacer un diccionario
> con una sola palabra (p. 295).

When they realize that it is actually Vivaldi's music, Silvestre says:
"—Chico—le dije—la cultura en el trópico. ¿Te das cuenta, mi viejo?"
(p. 298).

One of the many times Cué opens his mouth to talk, something strange happens:

> Iba a responder cuando oí que de mi boca salía un chorro de
> música: violento, incontenible, rítmico. Era un rocanrol que
> sonaba en alguna parte de la casa, debajo de mi asiento, creo....
> Creo que oí una voz humana por entre las guitarras eléctricas,
> los saxofones en celo y los aullidos de algún Elvis Presley
> traducido al español (p. 57).

Silvestre believes that where music begins words must die. Cué thinks that music is architecture in motion and makes comparisons between literature and music:

> La única literatura posible para mí, sería una literatura aleatoria.
> (¿Como la música? le pregunté.) No, no habría ninguna parti-
> tura, sino un diccionario...Quizá tuviéramos entonces verda-
> deros poemas y el poeta volvería a ser un hacedor o de nuevo un
> trovador (p. 331).

When the two friends hear a storm in the distance, they refer to the thunder as if it were an orchestral sound: "Un timbal lejano tocado con baqueta, dijo Héctor Berlioz Cué" (p. 405). This percussive reference returns us to the importance of rhythm in *Tres Tristes Tigres*. In music, as in pure rhythm, each note and each rhythmic beat is related to the other notes. Whether played simultaneously or in sequence, each note, as well as each silence between notes or beats, affects or changes the nature of whatever is around it. There are fine rhythms in the writing of *Tres Tristes Tigres*. For example, the writer composes the rhythm which La Estrella exudes by using a sequence of three adverbs: "Agitando el vaso a ritmo, rítmicamente, bella-mente, artísticamente ahora y el efecto total era una belleza tan

distinta, tan horrible, tan nueva..." (p. 64). The use of a series of
three adverbs, adjectives and so on, is very typical of the style of all
the book's narrators up to the final pages, where "Soltó el freno, salí"
(p. 443) is repeated three times, the reiteration of the preterite tense
accenting the finality of the phrase.

At times typographical oddities create an impression of silence:
black, blank or illegible pages (typed in reverse as in a mirror) or
drawings. Significantly, the word *silencio* appears often in *Tres Tristes
Tigres*, usually to indicate the end of something, as after Códac's
party. In Silvestre's final narration, *en silencio* is repeated thirty-three
times. The silence ushers in the dawn and with it the end of the
musical composition and Havana night life for Silvestre.

The unity of *Tres Tristes Tigres* may be said to be its musicality. The
true nature of music is, however, in Langer's interpretation:

> ... unconventionalized, unverbalized freedom of thought. ...
> The real power of music lies in the fact that it can be "true" to
> the life of feeling in a way that language cannot; for its
> significant forms have that *ambivalence* of content which words
> cannot have, [as well as] the possibility of expressing opposites
> simultaneously ... (p. 243).

Cabrera Infante's literary techniques, such as jumps in temporal
sequences, a lack of a clear-cut plot and a strong emphasis on
memories, in juxtaposition with word plays and rapid spatial movement of the characters, tend to approximate the simultaneity of
music. The content of *Tres Tristes Tigres* is ambivalent, as can be judged
by the great divergence in reader reactions and critical interpretations. The transcription of the phonetic quality of the spoken word
captures not only the various tones of Cuban dialects and speech
patterns, but also the feelings and mentality of the characters portrayed. The book succeeds in being the musical composition it
purports to be, given the limitations of the medium. And yet, the
literary form itself is a betrayal of the original voices and songs
orchestrated in the text, because "art—certainly music, and probably
all art," as Langer warns us, "is formally and essentially untrans-
latable" (p. 234).

II

Alhough the novel can approximate a musical composition in
content, tone and structure, the literary form in its essentially verbal

nature misrepresents the non-verbal quality of music. This tendency to deception is perpetrated by the "author's" concealment of the plot and by unreliable narrators who distract and confuse the reader in numerous ways. Códac, Eribó, Cué and especially Silvestre, all speak directly to the reader on many occasions, thus destroying the illusion of a world unto itself usually created in a fictional work. The reader is unable and unwilling to suspend his disbelief when dealing with a narrator who follows in the footsteps of Tristram Shandy. The narrators are also found to be unreliable in the sense that they often mix up time sequences, present only partial vignettes rather than episodes and generally cannot be trusted. As characters, they reveal a variety of treasonous attitudes, such as incipient self-betrayal, betrayal of literature for the movies, lying, delation or deceit and artifice as a life-style. The ephemeral and contradictory Bustrófedon is discussed as an intriguing example of the spirit of the Cuban *choteo* on an intellectual level, and is seen as reflecting the central problem of the book: language as betrayal. As my analysis of the character-narrators continues we find that a number of characteristics are shared by the several narrators, and Silvestre and Cué may be co-writers of the book. Most of the fictional beings in *Tres Tristes Tigres*, as characters and often as narrators, provide instances of the provocation and testing of betrayal as a reality of life.

Bustrófedon is somewhat of an enigma to both the characters and the readers of *Tres Tristes Tigres*. Códac begins "Rompecabeza" with:

> ¿Quién era Bustrófedon? ¿Quién fue quién será quién es Bustrófedon? ¿B? Pensar en él es como pensar en la gallina de los huevos de oro, en una adivinanza sin respuesta, en la espiral. *El era Bustrófedon para todos y todo para Bustrófedon era él* (p. 207).

The last sentence of this passage is quite obviously a literal play on the definition of Bustrófedon's name, the second half of the phrase being a reversal in order of all the words of the first half. The dictionary defines this word as follows:

> **boustrophedon:** *n.* An ancient method of writing in which the lines run alternately from right to left and from left to right, as in various ancient inscriptions in Egyptian, Greek, and certain other languages. *adj.* written in this way.[8]

---

[8] Clarence L. Barnhard, ed., *The World Book Dictionary* (Chicago: Doubleday and Co., 1972), p. 238.

The first references made to Bustrófedon are found in "Los debutantes" and in "Seseribo," when Eribó recognizes Bustrófedon's influence on his choice of words. Bustrófedon is present as a character at
Códac's party for La Estrella, where he carries a tray of drinks out of
the kitchen and is grabbed by Edith Cabell as she trips and falls. He is
heard inventing tongue twisters, and later asks Códac: "¿estás inflan-
do un globo?" (p. 125) when he hears La Estrella's snoring coming
from under the couch. His question sets off a humorous train of
thought in Códac. In "La casa de los espejos" Cué hears a voice
shouting: "Que sólo las lesbianas acaricien mi cara" (p. 139), which he
attributes to Bustrófedon, although he does not see him in the
crowd. A bit later he hears "una voz tal vez conocida que grita bien
claro 'Pa la posada'" (p. 143).

"Rompecabeza," Códac's narration centered around Bustrófedon,
begins with an anecdote about going to a restaurant with Bustrófedon and Rine. Besides the extensive exposure to anagrammatic games
and parodies of Martí and Darío, we learn a few things about the
character Bustrófedon: "él era un tipo largo y flaco y con muy mala
cara y esta malacara picada por el acne juvenil" (p. 209) and "tenía un
ojo malo, estrabiado...y siempre tenía dolores de cabeza, grandes,
enormes jaquecas" (p. 219). It seems that Cué, the first to see and
hear Bustrófedon, met him in New York where he had been influenced by the Argentinian dialect Lunfardo. When the doctors oper-
ated on Bustrófedon, it was to "quitarle los dolores de cabeza, los
vómitos de palabras, el vértigo oral, para eliminar de una vez y para
siempre...las repeticiones y los cambios y la aliteración o la alteración
de la realidad hablada..." (p. 222). Bustrófedon read only diction-
aries, which to him were better than any movie, dream or erotic
fantasy. He would search for palindromes and make wordplays with
any word or proper name imaginable. He gave everything a new
name as if he were actually inventing another language.

Although Cué criticizes the deceased Bustrófedon in "Bachata" for
his *grosería*, it may just be jealousy, for the same Cué supposedly said
that the recorded voices of the main characters in "Rompecabeza" are
parasite noises, "ruidos que son lo que fuimos nosotros de Bustrófedon" (p. 258). At least at that time Cué, like the others, tended to
deify Bustrófedon. Códac, for example, writes of Bustrófedon as "El"
(p. 270).

Bustrófedon's continual joking, his indecorous attitude towards literature and his astute parodies of the seven Cuban authors, all combine in our consideration of this character as the incarnation of a very Cuban phenomenon, the *choteo*, as discussed by Jorge Mañach in his *Indagación del Choteo*. The *choteo*, he says, consists of a habitual attitude of "no tomar nada en serio" or "Tirarlo todo a relajo.... Es cierto, pues, que el choteo ataca o esquiva por medio de la burla lo demasiado serio, si por tal se entiende lo que el choteador estima demasiado autorizado o ejemplar."[9] The *choteo* is neither *el humor* nor *la gracia*, but rather "una perversión de la burla." The independent and anti-hierarchical spirit of the Cuban reacts against a false, inflexible authority. The *choteo* devaluates, vulgarizes and makes familiar the exemplary, the "puffed-up."

Bustrófedon represents this spirit with regard to the conventions of language, both spoken and written, and especially with regard to the "sacred cows" of literary style. He never says anything in a conventional manner. Even though a few comprehensible sentences or questions can be attributed to Bustrófedon, they are either tongue-in-cheek comments or they include neologisms, or both. The usual is wordplay in which Bustrófedon is essentially making lists of words, such as palindromes or anagrams, which have onomatopoeic or associational values. He gives recitations of folkloric pieces (such as the "Cantata del Café"), of parodic variations of well-known poems and of his own creations, such as his "Diccionario de Palabras Afines y Ideas Sinfines."

The spirit of the *choteador* in Bustrófedon is clearly present in the various sections dedicated to his works: "Algunas revelaciones," "Los pro-y-contra nombres," and "La muerte de Trotsky referida por varios escritores cubanos, años después—o antes." In "Algunas revelaciones" Bustrófedon pricks the balloon of pomposity associated with a writer's having something in print. The written word is usually highly esteemed by the general populace, and perhaps even more so

---

[9] Jorge Mañach, *Indagación del Choteo*, 3rd ed. (Miami: Mnemosyne, 1969), p. 17. Reynaldo L. Jiménez devotes two chapters in his book *Guillermo Cabrera Infante y Tres Tristes Tigres* (Miami: Ediciones Universal, 1977) to the Cuban *choteo* as a point of departure for his analysis of *Tres Tristes Tigres*. In Chapter IV, "Actualización del choteo: Nivel anecdótico," he discusses the presence of humor in *Tres Tristes Tigres*, and in Chapter V, "Actualización del choteo: Nivel formal," he treats the deliberate ambiguity and fragmentation in the structure of the book as a function of the *choteo*.

by its author. So it is that the title preceding the blank pages prepares the reader for something impressive to follow. Bustrófedon reveals and deflates the self-aggrandizement of writers in three blank pages.

"Los pro-y-contra nombres," a scandalously hilarious listing of names of people who have been famous in the Western world, probably comes the closest to the typical *choteo* in its tendency to defame and devaluate. A few of these, from the list of "Bailarines" are:

Alicia Markova	La Stampa
Dix Entrechat	Jules Supermansky
Vaslav Vijinsky	Mijail Strogonoff
Vichinsky	Alicia Alonsova
Marx Platoff	(p. 267)

Even though the names are associated with cultural and intellectual giants, the distortion with which they are presented is reminiscent of name-calling, and reflects Mañach's intuitions:

> Pero el cubano es tan sincero—sincero hasta cuando miente, cosa que hace sin escrúpulos—que le repugna toda forma irónica de impugnación. Prefiere el choteo, que es la mofa franca, desplegada, nada aguda generalmente, como que no tiene hechura de dardo, sino más bien de polvillo de molida guasa, que se arroja a la cara de la víctima. El choteo la desconcierta, no por su contundencia, sino por el ambiente ahogador de alusiones, de equívocos, que va formando en torno a ella. (pp. 69-70)

This is not to overlook the highly intellectual nature of Bustrófedon's activities, which imply a broad knowledge of culture, literature and language, as well as a great facility with linguistic structures. The point I am making does not lower Bustrófedon to the level of the common *choteador* of yore, but rather elevates him as the embodiment of the spirit of the *choteo* on an intellectual plane, a fortunate blend of critical sensitivity and *relajo*.

The parodies of the seven Cuban writers preserved on tape by Códac represent the pinnacle of Bustrófedon's "works." A parody is usually a humorous imitation of a serious writing, but it is always a travesty of the original. For, while it may follow the form of its model, it changes the contents from sense to nonsense. Bustrófedon's parodies are treasonous of the writing style and theme of the specific works of the seven authors, but, unlike the translator, Bustrófedon distorts deliberately.[10] The harshest parody imitates the best known of the authors, Alejo Carpentier. This is only natural for the *choteador*, whose goal is to reduce the exemplary figure to his own level by openly mocking his style. As Carpentier is more esteemed he must be dealt with more radically, for he is the highest in the literary hierarchy which Bustrófedon wishes to abolish in carnivalesque spirit.

Returning to the spoken word, Bustrófedon is constantly involved with his word games, jokes and alteration of spoken reality. He is usually discussed by critics as the essence of living language, which indeed he is on one level, perhaps the most important. But he can also be treated as the oral tradition of folklore, since several folkloric pieces are attributed to him, including "Tres tristes tigres en un trigal..." and, as Códac says, the seven parodies belong to folklore. At the end of the seven parodies, Códac says he thinks Bustrófedon did the parodies as a lesson for Silvestre and Cué to the effect that literature is no more important than conversation. He then cites Bustrófedon as having said then and other times that "la única literatura posible estaba escrita en los muros... de los servicios públicos" and that "la otra literatura hay que escribirla en el aire" (p. 257), in other words, by talking. Bustrófedon contends that while traditional literature betrays the spontaneous orality it purports to represent, graffiti and talk are of the essence.

More than a master of parody, Bustrófedon is a character whose very existence exposes language and literature as betrayal. The most important things we know about this enigmatic anagrammatist are his attitudes about literature and how they correspond with his activities and his name. His constant alteration of the spoken word and his parodies of Cuban literature are distortions of those realities. As a champion of invisible writing, Bustrófedon inspires and at times perturbs his friends by an obsession with words in their pure and chaotic state. Words are the essence of speaking and writing, each equally important according to Bustrófedon. In spite of the fact that not just words, but also the conventions of written and spoken language, serve as the raw materials for communication, Bustrófedon

---

[10] For a good analysis of these literary parodies, see Vicki Gillespie Mickelsen, "Games Novelists Play: Technical Experiments in *La Muerte de Artemio Cruz, La Casa Verde, Tres Tristes Tigres,* and *Rayuela,*" Diss. Indiana University 1974, pp. 163-71.

is not concerned with these conventions, for he seems to have little interest in mundane or even rational discourse. He is rather, as described by Códac, the epitome of the surrealist metaphor: "[el doctor no sabía] que tenía sobre la mesa de operaciones, finalmente, el paraguas y la máquina de coser *punto* final" (p. 270). This passage from Lautréamont's *Les Chants de Maldoror* is written in the boustrophedon method in *Tres Tristes Tigres*. In the spirit of surrealism, whose fundamental tenets undermine conscious, rational activity, Bustrófedon represents the spontaneous flow of spoken language, as found in folklore or conversation, which dies when dissected.

In terms of conventional characterization, however, Bustrófedon's very name and the opinions he professes about literature reflect a psychotic personality split. His name is a word which describes a method of writing, and yet he refuses to leave any written work of his for posterity, going so far as to destroy the original tape of the seven parodies. His problem of identity is pointed out by Cué, who muses that of all the palindromes Bustrófedon found, he never came up with "el temible... Yo soy" (p. 358). In light of Bustrófedon's inherent self-betrayal and his anti-literature stance in a twentieth century novel, he is understandably a sad or trapped tiger, perhaps even *un gran contradictorio*.

Betrayal through lying is developed most extensively in "Seseribo," narrated by Silvio Sergio Ribot "de las actrices" (p. 325), a relatively poor *zambo* bongo player. He had been a commercial artist for while, until the outright lies about his marital and paternal status no longer helped him get a raise in pay. The night Eribó meets and falls for the desirable Vivian marks the beginning of a series of lies and misgivings amongst the tigers. Cué and Silvestre try to steer Eribó away from Vivian by repeating "Esa se acuesta" (p. 96) to him, while the music playing in the background is the bolero significantly entitled "Miénteme." Later, when Eribó and Vivian are on a date, Vivian tells him the secret of her self-betrayal, the loss of her virginity as an altruistic act. Although Eribó promises to keep the secret, saying "Seré una tumba" (p. 119), he does not, thus betraying her trust in him.[11] Eribó in turn is lied to by Cuba Venegas when he

---

[11] Eribó's response to Vivian is ambiguous. "Seré una tumba" is a popular expression used when one intends to keep a secret. *Tumba*, however, can be either a tomb or a type of drum: "La tumba (apócope de músicos para tumbadora) es una adaptación cubana de un tambor ritual africano" (3 May 1979).

asks her to go out after her show. She says she feels ill and wants to go right home after her performance. Later, when Eribó is waiting for Vivian, he sees Cuba Venegas with another man.

Códac's name is descriptive of his role in *Tres Tristes Tigres*: he is like a Kodak camera which acts as a witness, a camera's eye. Códac describes himself as "yo, este anónimo escriba de jeroglíficos actuales..." (p. 270) and is the narrator of "Rompecabeza" and the eight sections of "Ella cantaba boleros." He is a photo-journalist who works for a while on the night-club shows, where he meets La Estrella and other night creatures, until the censure is lifted again and he goes back to working on "la actualidad política" (p. 281). Códac speaks a bit of English and is a good friend of Bustrófedon, Rine Leal, Eribó, Silvestre and Cué. He is always involved in a superficial relationship with one or more women, including La Estrella, Cuba Venegas, Irenita and Maga. Silvestre attributes to Códac the saying that "En cada actor hay escondido una actriz" (p. 308), a coded way of referring to someone's being a failure, although it has other resonances that add color and ambiguity to the narrative.

While not a completely reliable narrator, Códac is relatively free from deceitful practices as a character. The only time he comes close to lying is when he coaxes La Estrella to his party under the pretext of an impressario's being there. When La Estrella discovers the deception, she refuses to sing. Códac wisely deceives Bustrófedon by preserving his copy of the tape, the original of which Bustrófedon had insisted on destroying.

He also provides us with several instances of the character-narrator speaking directly to the reader in the style of Tristram Shandy. He would like us to be able to hear the sound of the voices he is recording for us in writing: "(Lindo verdad? Pero había que oírlo.)" (p. 82); "(y este es uno de los pocos cubanos que pronuncia la segunda e del verbo creer, créanme)" (p. 84). On another occasion Códac admits to plagiarism: "(Linda frase ¿verdad? Lástima que no sea mía)" (p. 224). Several other times Códac's reliability as a narrator is questionable. In "Rompecabeza" it seems that Cué is part of the group, and yet in the very same long sentence Códac says that they found Arsenio in the Las Vegas Club avoiding them (p. 219). Then, in actions attributable to his drunken state in the seventh "Ella cantaba boleros," Códac's Cervantine narration jumps in time and space from one club and one night to another.

Unfaithful to his original goal of becoming a writer, Cué sold his soul to become an actor. In a rare moment of sincerity, Arsenio Cué tells Silvestre that he would not want to tell him what he had to do to get where he did in his career. Whatever it took, Cué became a very different person from the starving and unkempt Arsenio of "Los debutantes." He now possesses certain skills and personal refinements associated with his career. Nonetheless, he is currently, and once again, unemployed. An extremely pessimistic solitary type obsessed with death, speed and numbers, Cué is described for the most part by the other characters in negative terms. This is significant since they are supposedly his friends. Eribó finds him impatient and theatrically refined, and, after Vivian points it out, he notices that Cué has cold, cruel eyes which he usually hides behind sunglasses. While Cué's hatred for women makes it clear to him that "Las mujeres dicen siempre mentiras" (p. 432), Silvestre intimates to the reader that he is not all that trusting of Cué, who could just as well be lying as anyone else. Códac refers to "el rencor neurálgico de Arsenio Cué" (p. 223), who, in his educated voice, is always quoting "su rosario de citas" (p. 310) and at times cites sentences in Spanish "al revés" (p. 361). A compendium of Silvestre's unspoken comments about Cué suggests that he is not highly esteemed by his constant companion in "Bachata." In spite of their being "best" friends, the tigers regularly hide their true feelings and seem unable to communicate with each other. Silvestre compares Cué with "la ninfa hidrófila" (p. 412) for the narcissism they share, and refers to him variously as "el muy pedante elefantino" (p. 394), "un genio de la última palabra" (p. 350), "Dipsómano de la distancia" (p. 358), and "un neurótico del carajo" (p. 350). But Silvestre admires Cue's practical intelligence: "Recordé que también dento de él había un loro del pragmatismo: un locutor comercial" (p. 427).

Quick to agree that "Todo conduce a lo peor" (p. 400), Cué has a propensity for negative thinking which Silvestre calls his musical theme. Essentially a betrayal of his origins and himself, it includes diatribes against the country, people, music, Blacks, women, underdevelopment, everything. "Cuba...era solamente habitable para las plantas y los insectos y los hongos, para la vida vegetal o miserable" (p. 100). This pessimism is also reflected in Códac, although he is supposedly referring to Cuba Venegas: "es mejor, mucho mejor ver a Cuba que oírla y es mejor porque quien la ve la ama, pero quien la oye y la escucha y la conoce ya no puede amarla, nunca" (p. 278). Cué is a misogynist and speaks ill of women, except for Laura, for whom he may have felt love at some point. There is probably some truth to this interchange between him and Livia, a master of artifice:

[LIVIA]—Pero yo siempre he sido tu verdadero amor.
[CUÉ]—Sí digo desde el pasillo. El único, el último. (p. 156)

It seems that Silvestre is right when he says that Cué is in love with numbers and himself, for he certainly does not love Livia. Cué also has negative feelings about remembering, for his only memory is a painful one. Perhaps the reason for his constant quoting, enumerating and babbling on about almost any topic is to avoid the past by concentrating his thoughts on the present moment. The syntax which characterizes Cué lacks punctuation and relies heavily on the gerund: "—dijo Cué, caminando mirando gesticulando—" (p. 440) and "Me miró bizqueando gesticulando haciendo la mueca bucal de la E" (p. 442). These effects create the impression of the duration of an action in the present, faithfully reflecting Cué's life-style.

According to Códac, Silvestre is always trying to get Cué to write. When he asks Cué why he does not write, the latter says: "mejor, ¿por qué no traduzco?" (p. 311). This reflects Bustrófedon's view of literature as betrayal. Cué used to think he could write, but now he says he does not write because he has no "sentido de la historia" (p. 326). The only kind of literature Cué thinks would be possible for him is "una literatura aleatoria.... Quizá tuviéramos entonces verdaderos poemas y el poeta volvería a ser un hacedor o de nuevo un trovador" (p. 331).

Cué gave up writing for acting, but he does write his own story in the two sections of "Casa de los espejos," which illustrate concealment and secrecy amongst the friends, as well as unreliable narration. Part I, narrated in the past tense, describes Cué and Silvestre talking with Livia and Mirtila in the street. When Silvestre later shows an interest in Mirtila, Cué, who has little regard for her, dismisses the whole affair. We discover Cué was holding back information, for Part II is all about Livia and her friends. Cué says "Pude haberle dicho a Silvestre muchas cosas" (p. 146). Part II begins a few days later, with Cué going to visit these girls by himself. In the last four pages of Cué's narration, he displays inconsistency in his use of verbal tenses, as he switches indiscriminately from preterite or imperfect to the present tense.

Although he has a name , a profession and a future, Silvestre as the main character-narrator in *Tres Tristes Tigres* bears a resemblance to the no-longer-believed-in character that Nathalie Sarraute describes:

> ...a being devoid of outline, indefinable, intangible and invisible, an anonymous "I," who is at once all and nothing, and who as often as not is but the reflection of the author himself, has usurped the role of the hero, occupying the place of honor. The other characters, being deprived of their own existence, are reduced to the status of visions, dreams, nightmares, illusions, reflections, quiddities or dependents of this all-powerful "I."[12]

We know very little about Silvestre except for a few physical characteristics: "no soy fuerte, más bien soy gordo" (p. 398), his profession as writer, his friends and his love for the movies and for remembering: "me gusta acordarme de las cosas más que vivirlas..." (p. 297).

As the character-narrator of "Bachata," Silvestre, like Tristram, often speaks directly to the reader, explaining, apologizing or commenting, and regularly includes his thoughts and memories between the lines of dialogue. This element of his character is important because it exemplifies the narrator's disruptive role and his betrayal of the reader's expectations for a novel. Silvestre's narrative techniques seem to vary with his whim and at times he comments on this to the reader: "Dispenso al lector de la explícita bobería de los diálogos y le ofrezco en cambio las obras completas de Arsenio Cué. O mejor, su pandectas" (p. 321). Silvestre then describes what Cué is saying or doing: "(Pausa. Arsenio Wolfang Cuéthe dramatizaba sus palabras, segunda copa en mano)" (p. 322) and his own comments to Cué: "(Aquí cabe mejor tu Gran Venida, le dije. Se rió)" (p. 334).

Silvestre's manipulation of the conversation belies the greater manipulation he carries out in the whole book, exemplifying the strong authorial control of Menippean satire: "Decidí enlazar el fin con el principio, para que la conversación fuese feliz" (p. 342). A bilingual narrative sequence in XVII voiced by Silvestre suggests his having a hand in the Master of Ceremonies' monologue in the "Prólogo." Perhaps Silvestre is the book's Master of Ceremonies, as it

---

[12] Nathalie Sarraute, *The Age of Suspicion* (New York: Braziller, 1963), p. 56.

is he who records, compiles and presents its contents to the reader. Silvestre's technique changes erratically and without reason: on one page we find a solid paragraph filled with dialogue lines, and on the next page each dialogue line is given its own traditional line (pp. 340-41). A most obvious example of manipulation is the splitting up of Cué's story into two parts, followed by a reference to the page number earlier in the text where the first half is printed:

> .   Me lo contó todo. O casi todo. El cuento está en la página cincuenta y tres. Llegó a los disparos fatales. Hizo una pausa.... El final de la historia siguió por fin ahora. (p. 423)

Another narrative irregularity used by Silvestre and Cué to jolt the reader into an awareness of the artificiality of the novel is the confusion of verb tenses. By mixing up his temporal references, Silvestre makes it quite clear to us that he is writing about an experience at a time after the fact: "Se lo conté a Cué, entonces. Quiero decir, ahora" (p. 302), thus making the reader extremely aware of the devices the writer uses to draw us into his world. The narrator's uncertainty and indecision cause the reader to be unwilling and unable to suspend his disbelief. Some other examples of Silvestre's exposition of the writer's difficulty in maintaining temporal consistency are blunders such as: "Voy, fui a buscarlo" (p. 348), and "Algún día escribiré este cuento. Antes se lo conté así a Arsenio Cué" (p. 437).[13] The P.S. at the end of the note from GCI suggests that Silvestre may be unreliable, or at least tardy, on his job: "PS, No olvides escribirme la nota de presentación a tiempo. Recuerda lo que pasó la semana pasada. El Dire echaba Fab...por la boca" (p. 439). When Silvestre found the forgotten note crumpled up in his pocket it was already the wee hours of the morning, and, as we know, he did no work for at least a day or so after that time. Silvestre's faltering memory adds to the reader's difficulty in taking him seriously: "(Eso es literatura. ¿Le dije?) (p. 330); "¿Qué dije?" (p. 348); "le dije pero no

---

[13] The latter example is more complex: the reference in the preterite tense is to the story just narrated to Cué (pp. 436-37). The sentence written in the future tense refers to the story which Silvestre was telling to Cué, as that is the verbal tense Silvestre was using at the end of the of the story. Another version of the story, which is quite different, appears in "Los debutantes" (pp. 41-42). The discrepancies between the two tellings of the experience serve to question Silvestre's memory and his reliability as a narrator.

me oyó. ¿O fue que no lo dije?" (p. 358). This tendency adds to his unreliability as a narrator and underscores the difficulties inherent in remembering in contrast to memorizing, Cué's specialty. Other comments show off his bi-lingual ability—"I laughed. Digo, me reí" (p. 374)—but confound the Spanish-speaking reader.

The relationship between Silvestre and Cué is a puzzling one which I believe is central to *Tres Tristes Tigres*, especially as a manifestation of various types of betrayal. Many indications are given to imply that these characters represent two sides of the same coin, and may even be co-writers of the book, thus leading us to consider the themes of identity and of the "double." Silvestre, as the main writer, may safely be assumed to be the author's mask or *persona*, and the other main character-narrators may be the variants or alternate characteristics of that same *persona*:

> A story told in the first person satisfies the legitimate scruples of the author. In addition, it has the appearance, at least, of real experience and authenticity, which impresses the reader and dispels his mistrust.
>
> For nobody today is entirely misled by the convenient procedure that consists, for the novelist, in parsimoniously apportioning bits of himself, which he invests with a certain likelihood by dividing them...among his characters. By a process of decortication, the reader then removes these bits and places them, as in a game of lotto, in corresponding compartments he has discovered in himself.
>
> Today, everybody is well aware, without being told, that "la Bovary—c'est moi." (From Flaubert's correspondence.) And since the important thing now, rather than to extend indefinitely the list of literary types, is to show the co-existence of contradictory emotions and to reproduce as closely as possible the wealth and complexity of the world of the psyche, the writer, in all honesty, writes about himself (Sarraute, pp. 66-67).

While our main concern is with "Silvestre Ycué" (in Códac's words, p. 222) "el dúo" (in Eribo's terms, p. 107), Silvestre himself realizes that a very thin line separates himself and the other personalities or styles: "(¿Por qué este mimetismo? Siempre termino siendo lo que los otros: díganme cómo hablo y les diré quién soy, que es como decir con quién ando)" (p. 295). Here he finds himself copying Cué's style, identifying too much with him, although he suggests that this happens with whomever he comes in contact. Although Silvestre shares Códac's love for the past and remembering, his most frequent companion is Cué, and "Viajar con Cué es hablar, pensar, asociar como Cué..." (p. 293). Silvestre recognizes and points out the resemblances among the characters' obsessions:

> [Cué] estaba recorriendo la palabra kilómetro y pensé que su intención era pareja a mi pretensión de recordarlo todo o a la tentación de Códac deseando que todas las mujeres tuvieran una sola vagina...o de Eribó erigiéndose en el sonido que camina o el difunto Bustrófedon que quiso ser el lenguaje. Eramos totalitarios: queríamos la sabiduría total, la felicidad, ser inmortales al unir el fin con el principio. Pero Cué se equivocaba (todos nos equivocamos, todos menos, quizás, Bustrófedon que ahora podía ser inmortal), porque si el tiempo es irreversible, el espacio es irrecorrible y además, infinito (pp. 317-18).

The characters in conjunction can be seen as an attempt on the part of the author to immortalize an epoch in Havana. In this sense, the city itself may be considered the central character of the book, as William H. Gass ascribes the function of a character to "anything which serves as a fixed point."[14] Silvestre and Cué represent the desire to return in time and space to that epoch, Eribó to its music and Códac to its women, as the latter tries to capture the essence of it all in a photograph. The spoken language of the epoch (Bustrófedon) is immortalized in *Tres Tristes Tigres*. The desires of the others unite them in frustration up against the unattainable. Even Cué is described at times as being similar to the others in language and writing style. He was known, for instance, to go through some changes when he drank a certain amount of alcohol: "La bebida devolvía a Cué a los orígenes. Ahora hablaba en el dialecto popular de Códac y Eribó y Bustrófedon a veces" (p. 342), removing some of his facade and his "voz educada por el aire." Despite Cué's preoccupation with numbers and his being the one to coin the phrase that "Everything happens in three's" (p. 155), the use of three adjectives, three prepositional phrases, three gerunds, or any such combination of three words creating a balanced rhythm, appears to be a stylistic

[14] William H. Gass, *Fiction and the Figures of Life* (New York: Knopf, 1970), p. 50.

model, fashioned by the title, for virtually every narrator in *Tres Tristes Tigres*, including at times Maga and Laura.

In "Confesiones de un comedor de gofio cubano" we are given to believe that Silvestre and Cué are collaborating as writers. This is an interesting possibility in light of their being apparently opposite "types" and Cué's being Silvestre's "double." Silvestre, referring to himself, footnotes the first italicized title: "Los titulitos pertenecen, por supuesto, al anotador" (p. 322). Cué tells Silvestre "anota" (p. 323) in the middle of one of his sentences, and a bit later in the same section ("Bachata" XI) he says: "Si quieres añade algo de T.S. Eliot (casi dijo Teselio), como Time present and time past o esa cita de Gertrude Stein, que es tu favorita" (p. 334). In "Bachata" XX, the following interchange suggests that Cué is reading parts of the book which Silvestre has already written:

[CUÉ]—Eres tú un contradictorio?
[SILVESTRE]-Es una figura de retórica.
 —¿Quién? ¿Marlowe o tú?
 —Mi manera de hablar.
 —Ten cuidado. Las maneras de hablar son también modos de escribir. Terminarás haciendo figuras con la retórica, pajaritas de papel impreso, garabatos et caetera.
 —¿Tú crees también que la retórica es culpable de la mala literatura? Es como achacarle a la física la caída de los cuerpos.
 Pasó la página con la mano en vuelo repetido (p. 418).

But Silvestre's poor memory causes him an embarrassing moment when he lies to Cué:

[CUÉ]—¿No irías a escribir esto ahora?
[SILVESTRE]—No, que va. Hace rato que no escribo (p. 404).

After this, Cué indirectly indicates to Silvestre that he knows his statement to be false. Silvestre's response prompts a barrage of references to their relationship:

[SILVESTRE]—Cabrón, ¿quién te enseñó el recorte?
[CUÉ]—Tú. Silvestre the First, el que llegó primero, yo-lo-dije-antes-que-Adán, el descubridor que vio a Cuba (Venegas) antes que Cristoforibot, el primer hombre en la luna, el que lo enseña todo aun antes de aprenderlo, el Singular, Top Banana, el uno de Plotino, Adán, Nonpareil, el Antiguo, Ichi-ban, Número Uno, Unamuno. Salve. Yo, el Dos, el Yang de tu Yin, Eng de tu Chan, el Gran Paso, el Discípulo, el Plural, Number Two, Second

Banana, Dos Passos, el 2, te saludo, ya que voy a morir. Pero no
quiero morir solo. Sigamos siendo, como dijo el iluminado Códac, los gemelos, los Jimaguas ñáñigos de Eribó, dos amigos y
ven conmigo. (pp. 404-05)

Silvestre deceives his buddy in other ways as well, especially through
the sin of omission. Ever fearful of Cué's cleverness, Silvestre
hesitates to say what is really on his mind: "Debí haberle dicho que....
Pero no dije nada" (p. 305), and later, "Ah coño—dije yo y pensé, Al
carajo, otro tigre con rayas infinitas, pero dije: —Un cabalista" (p. 312).
The implications of Silvistre and Cué as co-writers are carried to a
more complex level in a discussion of their friendship and the theme
of the double.

III

Thematic elements in *Tres Tristes Tigres* include a variety of topics
which center around love and the recurring motif of betrayal.
Women are characterized as sex objects, and major characters are
involved in love triangles and in friendships, with betrayal in love and
friendship as the main theme. Characters betray themselves, their
origins and especially each other, through lies, secrets, delation,
falsity and pretence. After a look at the secondary female characters,
I describe the two major love triangles and the characterization of La
Estrella and Laura Díaz, and finally examine Cué's narcissism in
terms of his friendship with Silvestre and the theme of the double.

Women in *Tres Tristes Tigres* are generally considered deceptive,
untrustworthy and unreliable. As a result they are usually treated
with little respect. Cuba Venegas, formerly Gloria Pérez, was discovered by Eribó and subsequently is associated with numerous other
lovers on her climb to success. In Delia Doce's letter we learn of
Cuba's humble beginnings and her facile self-betrayal. She had become more and more disloyal to her origins and her natural self, as
exemplified by her change of name, her new appearance and manners
and her carousing with both men and women.

Magalena Crus also breaks bonds with her past, wanting to live in
the present moment, to have a good time. Maga belies an interest in
other women: "quien te dijo, dígole, que el casnaval e un hombre,
ademá bailal no e delito, dígole..." (p. 34). Maga trades in her
innocence for a rather dubious life-style. Arsenio finds her at the TV
magnate's house when she is only fourteen or fifteen, apparently as a

mistress to the rich man. She is eighteen or nineteen when he again meets her in the company of Beba, one of Livia's cohorts, when he and Silvestre pick them up for a night on the town in "Bachata." This pair, Maga and Beba, seem to be totally lacking in culture and are referred to by Silvestre as "fieras nocturnas" (p. 398), "un dúo" (p. 371) easier to make love to than to make laugh. In this sequence of pure *machismo*, Cué says: "Esas mujeres no se presentan, se regalan" (p. 364). Maga is described as a "tremenda mulata" (p. 364) who has gone crazy. Cué attributes a spot on her nose to hysteria. Beba "no es mulata, pero un mestizaje sutil.... Tenía el pelo negro, largo, recién peinado ahora y ojos grandes, redondos, maquillados y una boca que más que sensual era depravada, como se dice" (p. 369).

In a phone call to Livia in "Los debutantes," Beba shows that her life-style revolves around betrayal and deceit. Despite her introduction at the Tropicana Club as Arabella Longoria de Suárez Dámera, she is not married to her escort, nor is she "bella y gentil y elegante" (p. 18). Beba is telling Livia, her former roommate, that she and Cipriano may have to get married due to his social position. But whether they do or not, she will continue to cheat on this man who is keeping her: "Sí claro que yo tengo cuidado. El ni se ocupa, bobita.... No, si él me deja, porque él sabe bien a mí no se me puede amarrar corta" (p. 45). She is even learning to drive for clandestine reasons.

Beba claims to be Maga's aunt. But during a romantic tryst with Silvestre on the beach, Maga cries and behaves in a disturbing manner, accusing Beba of keeping her locked up and of beating and abusing her. Silvestre takes pity on Maga and wants to help her. Cué, who thinks he knows people better, is amazed at Silvestre's naiveté and advises him to forget her.

Irenita and Ingrid are two more ladies of the night world who are described solely in terms of their physical attributes and willingness or unwillingness to make love with tigers such as Códac and Silvestre. Irenita with her siren-like qualities quickly becomes lost in a sea of embraces with Códac soon after meeting him. In a cheap motel Silvestre plays along with Ingrid's pretences of propriety in various stages of undress. He awakens with shock to a wig on the pillow and a completely bald companion, witness to the stark reality behind the deceptive appearances of Havana women at night.

Two incomplete stories of frustrated love provide partial plot lines

to *Tres Tristes Tigres*. Since the traditional novel has a substantial plot
in which the reader may become engrossed, the notable lack of plot in
Tres Tristes Tigres heightens the impression of fragmentation. It also
makes feasible the type-casting of characters. As in Menippean satire,
the characters are flat and superficial. Because the love triangles
provide for potentially meaningful character interaction, it is important to observe the scanty plot line associated with them. The first
love story focuses on Vivian Smith-Corona, a wealthy and beautiful
criolla of sixteen years who is a desirable sexual object to the friends.
She is introduced to Eribó by Silvestre, a fourth party who squares
the triangle as a negative go-between. Vivian is characterized as a
fresh young socialite who seems to fall for Eribó, but perhaps she
does so only to make Cué jealous. This is plausible given that the
latter claims to have gone to bed with her and yet is dating her
girlfriend, Sibila. Silvestre initiates his infamous line, "Esa se acuesta,"
presumably to discourage Eribó from getting interested in Vivian.
Vivian subsequently uses Eribó to tell him of her loss of virginity, but
has no intentions of getting serious with him. Silvestre is not directly
involved, but is curious as to whether or not Cué did in fact go to bed
with Vivian. All of the interactions are plagued with insincerity,
mistrust and manipulation in the guise of love and friendship.

Cué, Livia, Laura (Laurilivia) and Silvestre are involved in the
major love triangle of the book. Cué often describes the enticing Livia
and her various roommates as looking exactly alike. Livia has inspired
women such as Mirtila, Laura Díaz and Beba to transform themselves, as she has done, into glamorous images of fashion and make-
up. Cué met Laura through Livia before she became a top fashion
model. From that day he maintained a sort of awe of Laura, due
originally to his first impression of her in a state of natural beauty.
But as time passed this awe continued, since Laura seems to posses
an integrity lacking in the other females of Cué's fan club. Despite
his falling in love with Laura, he becomes ensnared by Livia's trap of
exhibitionism and betrayal, finally losing Laura. Livia reminds Cué
that she has always been his true love. The fact that the reader does
not know any of the details which lead from Cué and Laura's
breaking up to Silvestre's announcement of marriage to Laura inten-
sifies the schism between the typical characterization of novels and
the "types" that we find in *Tres Tristes Tigres*.

That females are, for the most part, viewed as sexual objects in

Tres Tristes Tigres reflects the *machismo* which is part and parcel of Havana night life in the 1950's. The only women who go beyond this stereotype are La Estrella and Laura Díaz. The success story of La Estrella is based on her real and natural talent. Códac was attracted to her as a cosmic phenomenon, and La Estrella was hurt by his lack of interest in her as an individual woman. While she betrayed Códac only in minor ways, such as the story about El Bobo, her invalid son, she was herself gravely betrayed by the contract she signed on her rise to fame. La Estrella could not read the fine print which required that she sing with accompaniment.

Laura, on the other hand, is a narrator in her own right, and thus is the only female who expresses herself in her own words. She narrates the eleven psychiatric sessions as well as the first vignette of "Los debutantes." Some of the sessions are dreams, which leads one to believe that the dream Silvestre recounts in "Bachata" must have been Laura's. Through Laura's narrations we learn that she came from a small town, later became an actress and is now married to a writer who is "Muy culto..., muy ingenioso..., muy inteligente..." (p. 71). She no longer acts on the stage and seems to have an identity problem which is her motivation for seeking psychiatric help. She has a daughter from a previous marriage, although the facts surrounding these events are cloudy, since Laura at times admits to lying to the doctor. Laura's most troubling problem seems to be her identification with a childhood friend who may be her double. In "Los debutantes" she and a friend tattle on Petra and her boyfriend, as an act of retaliation, because Petra's mother was going to report their doings to their mothers. The little girls were afraid someone would find out what they were really doing under the truck, so they capitalized on scandalizing Petra in order to hide their own escapades: "Pero siempre Aurelita y yo hacíamos cositas debajo del camión" (p. 24). Their spreading the story succeeded in breaking up the relationship between Petra and her boyfriend and in disgracing Petra and her mother. Laura later sees a childhood friend who is a kitchen maid at a rich boyfriend's house (Fifth Session) and, out of shame, refuses to recognize her. In the last session Laura describes the violation of a friend by the baker back in the small town, but at this point she is not sure whether it was herself or her friend who was violated!

Laura does not belong to Havana's night life, nor to the actual world of the tigers. Her narration in "Los debutantes" as Aurelita is a childhood memory, and may be yet another psychiatric session. The events in that vignette took place previous to the action of *Tres Tristes Tigres*, and the sessions take place after it. Present in the tigers' world only as a memory to Cué and as a future wife to Silvestre, Laura symbolizes the ominous potential for true love and a meaningful relationship, neither of which exists in their world. Perhaps her presence is felt most keenly in her dream, as told by Silvestre, of the destruction of Havana by an apocalyptic explosion. She indeed represents a portentous unknown, the end of life in Havana as the friends now know it. Silvestre will no longer be a roving night creature after his marriage to Laura, and Cué will be without his friend.

Let us now examine the nature of this friendship which contains all the essential ingredients of the double as a literary theme, with rivalry in love precipitating the ultimate betrayal. In Otto Rank's study of this type of pathology, he states that "the mental conflict creates the double which corresponds to a projection of inner turmoil."[15] Characteristics of the doubles theme in literature, and applicable to the characters in *Tres Tristes Tigres*, are, in Rank's terminology, "a narcissistic disposition," "rivalry in love," "a defective capacity for love," "paranoid ideas of pursuit" and "thanatophobia."

Cué is already notorious for looking at himself in the mirror, although "Narciso Cué" claims his purpose is not what it may seem to be: "no me miro para ver si estoy bien o mal, sino solamente para saber si soy. Si sigo ahí. No sea que haya otra persona dentro de mi piel...Estoy. Pero ¿soy?" (p. 349). Just as a double usually looks like his creator, so do Silvestre and Cué look alike:

[MAGA]—Son igualitos, raros los do (p. 395).

[IRENITA]—Uy si son iqualitos...Pero los amo a los dos (p. 412).

Discussing their identity with each other is a favorite topic. Silvestre proposes they impersonate the presocratic dúo Damon and Pitias, philosophers of the fourth century B.C. who were famous for the friendship which united them. Although it may be just another word game to them, Silvestre and Cué are quite explicit about their identification with each other:

---

[15] Otto Rank, *The Double: A Psychoanalytic Study* (Chapel Hill: University of North Carolina Press, 1971), p. 76. The categories used in my discussion of the theme of the double in literature are summarized from Rank, pp. 71-77.

> [SILVESTRE]—Lo cierto es que ni tú ni yo somos contradictorios. Somos idénticos, como dijo tu amiga Irenita.
> [CUÉ]—¿La misma persona? Una binidad. Dos personas y una sola contradicción verdadera (p. 419).

It is difficult for the reader to take the dúo seriously at this point, since it appears that they lack the closeness necessary for a sincere friendship. As Jonathan Tittler has found, the rules of the verbal games played by the characters in *Tres Tristes Tigres* tend to alienate and isolate them from each other; specifically, by choosing the wrong antecedent to a referent when given a choice, and by talking on a subject of which one character is ignorant, keeping him in the dark as long as possible.[16] But to some extent this behavior supports the hypothesis of the double, since, according to Erik H. Erikson, "the development of psychosocial intimacy is not possible without a firm sense of identity,"[17] and the lack of a sense of identity is the root of the problem in the pathology of the double. If the sense of identity were strong enough, the split would not occur. In line with this theory we might examine the opposing views on remembering held by Silvestre and Cué as symptomatic of such a split. While their attitudes would seem to differentiate these characters at a deep level, Julio Matas observes that Silvestre's fondness for remembering (*recordar*) and Cué's proclivity for memorizing (*memorizar*) are really just "opuestos complementarios... dos funciones de la memoria difícilmente separables."[18] Although Cué insists that he is not a double: "No soy un doppelgänger. Soy mi imagen del espejo" (p. 400), this equivocal reference to being his image in the mirror is echoed in one of Silvestre's utterances:

> (Critiqué aquí—yo entre todas las personas: pero siempre soy así: reacciono contra lo que tengo enfrente, aunque sea mi imagen del espejo—, le censuré que se llevara de tal manera por los números y me respondió recitando:) (p. 330).

16 J. Tittler, "Intratextual Distance in *Tres Tristes Tigres*," *Modern Language Notes*, 93 (1978), 289.

17 Erik H. Erikson, *Identity: Youth and Crisis* (New York: W. W. Norton, 1968), p. 186.

18 Julio Matas, "Orden y Visión de *Tres Tristes Tigres*," *Revista Iberoamericana*, 40 (1974), 95.

The uncanny suggestion is that Cué and Silvestre see each other as a mirror image.

Rank believes that "Actually, and considered externally, the double is the rival of his prototype in anything and everything, but primarily in the love for woman...a trait which he may partly owe to the identification with the brother" (p. 75). There is a decided rivalry between Silvestre and Cué regarding Vivian and Laura. The games of verbal deception, the withholding of information from each other, the continual game of one-upmanship that dominates the relationship, all point to a deep-seated rivalry between Silvestre and Cué. When Silvestre says: "en cada actor hay escondido una actriz" (p. 308) he gravely upsets Cué, for it is an indirect way of telling Cué that he knows the story of his having loved and lost Laura.

Cué shares several qualities with Dorian Gray, with whom Silvestre compares him at one point, and whose description by Rank is reminiscent of Cué:

> Tied in with this narcissistic attitude is his imposing egoism, his inability to love, and his abnormal sexual life. The intimate friendships with young men...are attempts to realize the erotic infatuation with his own youthful image. From women he is able to obtain only the crudest sensual pleasures, without being capable of a spiritual relationship. Dorian shares this defective capacity for love with almost all double-heroes (Rank, pp. 71-72).

Cué is too self-centered to be able to love. Silvestre's announcement of marriage to Laura thus marks the definitive defeat of Cué in the game of love.

While paranoia does not have a substantial exemplar in *Tres Tristes Tigres*, to the outside observer it may seem that Cué acts as if he were being pursued. In his continuous and interminable driving around he identifies himself and is identified by Silvestre as *being* speed and velocity. On one occasion, however, Silvestre intimates that the idea of *fuga* must be in Cué's mind (p. 320). Also, the dream Cué has, in which he is by the sea with everyone running away, leads us to the conclusion that he is indeed being pursued by something in his obsessive search for time in space.

Cué seems to experience paranoia with regard to death, and perhaps he suffers from thanatophobia, an abnormal fear of death. In the literature of the double, the fear of aging, an offshoot of narcissism and a form of death, drives the character to suicidal tendencies. It is not death itself, insists Rank, but "the *expectation* of the unavoidable destiny of death [that] is unbearable to them" (p. 77). Death, "El Bulldozer de Dios," is one of the topics in Cué's pandectus. To Cué, life is only inertia and propaganda, whereas death transforms our lives into destinies. Many of Cué's comments foreshadow an obsessive worry about death: "Moraleja: Todos los hombres son mortales, pero algunos hombres son más mortales que otros" (p. 335). He equates his car with death, "su máquina invisible" (p. 334), which will find its visual incarnation in *Vanishing Point* (1972), Cabrera Infante's film script written under the pseudonym Guillermo Cain. Cué seems to believe he will one day have an accident and die. The fact that Cué does not like change is a possible variation of not wanting to grow old. He becomes extremely nervous when Silvestre speaks of the realities of death, for instance, of Bustrófedon's death (p. 403).

Of especial interest to the characterization of Silvestre and Cué are the parallelisms between the duo and the story of Cholo and his rival, and these will lead up to my concluding comments on Silvestre and Cué. Silvestre tells the story as a naive exercise in nostalgia, but Cué interprets it as an analogy to the relationship between himself and Silvestre, identifying Silvestre as Cholo, and himself as the dead rival who had in fact drawn and shot first, thus instigating his own demise. Cué offers a toast "a la buena suerte y mejor puntería de Cholo" (p. 437). The key to their previously symbiotic relationship lies in the symbolism of light and dark. Silvestre says: "Nos reímos. Es evidente que teníamos nuestras claves del alba y del ocaso" (p. 310). Silvestre represents re-birth or renewal, a new beginning, literally "un nombre de niña (no lo entendí: clave del alba)" (p. 445) which refers, of course, to Aurelita at the start of *Tres Tristes Tigres*, Laura as a child. Cué, on the other hand, prefigures decadence or ending, thus his death. A girl had once said she was going to show him the morning star, but it turned out to be a dirty light bulb:

> Me enseñó una luz. Venus, me dijo, el Lucero del Alba. Lo grave no es que fuera al anochecer ni el fiasco erótico, sino que miré y vi solamente un bombillo brillando amarillo y soez en una azotea (p. 327).

In terms of the double Silvestre has found love and a new sense of inner unity, no longer having need of his projected other self who did the driving, literally and figuratively speaking. Early in "Bachata" it is

intimated that Silvestre does not know how to drive, but now he says
to Cué that he is ready to take his place at any time (p. 362). In other
words, he is prepared to take control of his own life. As a fellow
character, Silvestre betrays Cué in love. As a writer he betrays their
friendship in literature:

> ¿Quién va a traicionar a su patria o a su matria ...para
> conservar un amigo, cuando sabe que puede traicionar a los
> amigos y mantenerlos en conserva como peras pensantes?
> Arsenio Del Monte...la cubanidad es amor...Silvestre Libbys
> (p. 443).

Silvestre's final narration closes with the neologism *Tradittori*, a
word formed by combining the Italian refrain: *Traduttore, traditore*
"translator, traitor," meaning that all translation betrays the original.
The immediate reference in *Tres Tristes Tigres* would seem to be to
Lino Novás Calvo's translation of Hemingway's *The Old Man and the
Sea*, in which he poorly translates "lions" as *morsas* 'walruses'. Silvestre
and Cué discuss this topic on page 341. Silvestre's reference to page
101, however, is vague. Does it refer to Novás Calvo's translation or
to *Tres Tristes Tigres*? Should it be the latter, the reference offers yet
another dimension to our perception of the novel. On page 101 Eribó
and Vivian are talking while Cué, who supposedly came to the pool
to see Vivian, is talking with a group of girls whose feet are dangling
in the water, "su harán de húmedas fanáticas" (p. 101). The suggestion of a cross reference to these water nymphs as "sea-morsels"
(p. 445) by Silvestre allows the reader to conjecture once more as to
this narrator's role in *Tres Tristes Tigres*. If indeed he does mean page
101 of *Tres Tristes Tigres*, Silvestre is definitely Cabrera Infante's
persona, for this page in the "Seseribo" section is narrated by Eribó,
and the only characters present at that time are Eribó, Cué and
Vivian. Silvestre would not be able to refer to that incident were he
not the "author" of the book, responsible for the creation of these
characters, their dialogues and dramas.[19]
    Cabrera Infante's comments on *Tres Tristes Tigres*'s thematic nu-

---

[19] This hypothesis does not contradict my statements about the theme
of the double in *Tres Tristes Tigres*, for just as an author can unfold various
aspects of his personality among several characters in a novel, so too can
the author's *persona* fulfill this function in the book he writes and compiles.

cleus, "treason in language, literature and love," as well as the key neologism *Tradittori*, prompted this study of betrayal in the medium (language), form (literature), and theme (love) of the book. The written word betrays the spoken word by freezing its fluidity and removing its accompanying gestures and tone. Translation from one langauge to another, as evidenced in "Los visitantes," or from one art form to another results in inaccuracy and distortion. Literature is travestied by translation and parody. In short, *Tres Tristes Tigres* is dedicated to self-exposure. The novel sets off a chain reaction effect, beginning with the betrayal implicit in the use of words to represent the objects and feelings of an individual's "reality." In the process, an important part of the reader's assumptions about literature, which enable him to suspend his disbelief, has been severely jostled by *Tres Tristes Tigres*:

> [I]t must be assumed for the purpose of fiction that non-verbal experience can be verbalized, that language is a fixed and exact form of expression which has the same denotations and connotations for the writer and reader alike, that a sequential medium can express simultaneous effects, and that a discrete medium can express flow (Mendilow, p. 50).

Characterization in *Tres Tristes Tigres* is at the service of the labyrinth of deceptive and treasonous attitudes towards oneself and others which are the essence of the anecdotal and thematic materials. Following in the Menippean tradition, the book provides for the provocation and testing of a problematic issue of human concern.

❧ 4 ❧

Cinema and Sex in the City:
La Habana Para Un Infante Difunto

A Habana para un Infante Difunto, originally entitled *Las confesiones de agosto,* is classified as a novel by the publisher. But Cabrera Infante has said he will resort to this nomenclature only to be eligible for a literary prize.[1] Indeed, until studied within the Menippean tradition, *Tres Tristes Tigres* and *La Habana* seem to defy categorization. Both works are saturated with menippea, from oxymoron, wordplay and parody, to characterization by types and the "dialogical attitude."[2] The more scabrous elements of Menippean satire present in *La Habana,* such as "underworld naturalism" and "scandalous, eccentric behavior," can be attributed

---

[1] *La Habana Para Un Infante Difunto* (Barcelona: Seix Barral, 1979). In a presentation at New York University, 17 April 1980, Cabrera Infante discussed this, his most recent book as of this publication, written in London, 1975-78.

[2] In *Dostoevsky's Poetics* (Ann Arbor: Ardis, 1973) Mikhail Bakhtin discusses "dialogical relationships" in the metalinguistic phenomena of "stylization, parody, *skaz* and dialog," in all of which "the word has a double-directedness—it is directed both toward the object of speech, like an ordinary word, and toward *another word,* toward *another person's speech*" (p. 153).

not only to the absence of Spanish censorship in 1979, but also to the maturity of a writer who has given free reign to a brilliant albeit audacious literary talent.

The word play begins with the title, a parody of a work for the piano by Maurice Ravel, *Pavane pour une infante défunte*. It is important to note here that in the text the narrator refers to the composer Ravel as an imitator, a parodist, a poet of pastiche, in other words a man after the author's own heart. The absence of *pavane* in the title may suggest its occurrence or reflection in the stucture of the book. The pavane is a slow, processional dance of the late Renaissance, which winds slowly forward, although steps may also be taken backward. A similar pattern is seen in the temporal progression in the novel, which, while mostly linear, occasionally reverts to the focal point of the first chapter, "La casa de las transfiguraciones." In a variation of the dignified dance, the procession divides with partners separating, circling the room and then rejoining. This recurring motif of seeking one's other half culminates in the phantasmagorical adventure at the end of the book, when an alluring woman who is entering a movie theatre invites the narrator with suggestive body language "al vals de la vida" (p. 690).

Once again, the content of the work consists of "the adventures of an *idea*," only this time it centers on erotic love. On several occasions the narrator gets off the subject of his love life and starts digressing on politics, culture or school days, but he quickly rectifies the situation and returns to his erotic strategies:

> Pero no es de política ni de cultura ni aun de política cultural que hablo sino del amor y de sus formas y de las formas de mi amor, aun de las formas vacías de amor (p. 312).

He discusses the contradictions of love, its vulgarity, stupidity and illogical nature. He describes it as degenerating from chess to poker, and the writer names the phases of love: "(una historia de amor siempre se repite: primero como comedia, luego como tragicomedia)" (p. 244). This pattern is most applicable to the affairs engaged in by the narrator, whose lifestyle and memories provide the focus for *La Habana*, an amusing treatise on *machismo*.

Following some introductory comments on the cinematic elements in *La Habana* and a synopsis of the book, this chapter will discuss the narrator's role as a writer and the theme of *machismo* in *La Habana*.

I

Throughout Cabrera Infante's works we are aware of the presence of the cinema, explicitly in *Un oficio del siglo XX* and *Arcadia todas las noches*, and implicitly in his novels *Tres Tristes Tigres* and *La Habana*. The far-reaching influence of the cinema on Cabrera Infante is evidenced in his works through a greater emphasis on space, place and movement than on chronology, a thematic obsession with the transitory nature of memories, personality and life, and at times an express intent to make a book a movie. The sense of space inherent in film, and achieved through movement, is simulated superficially in the action of *Tres Tristes Tigres* by the characters' driving around Havana, and in *La Habana* by the narrator's ambulating from one movie theatre or *posada* to another. Upon close analysis, however, it becomes clear that spatialization and cinematic movement permeate Cabrera Infante's vision and are made manifest in his writings as verbal and visual vanishing points, such as memories and experiments with the theme of the double. In both film and fiction Cabrera Infante's personalistic impulse finds expression in a preoccupation with remembering and selfhood, developed creatively within a spatial framework through dialogues with the past, the doubles theme, and death.

Numerous critics have cited the cinema as a model for Cabrera Infante's writing. Josefina Ludmer asserts that *Tres Tristes Tigres* "trata de reproducir... la totalidad de las imágenes visuales y auditivas," and "la sociedad del texto reproduce un equipo técnico de filmación, con su escritor-guionista (Silvestre), sus actores principales (Cué y Laura), su fotógrafo (Códac), la música (Eribó y La Estrella)."[3] While *Tres Tristes Tigres*, "a gallery of voices," is oriented towards a sound track, *La Habana* is a "museo de mujeres," a bazaar of bodies, with relatively little dialogue. The emphasis is now on the visual, the tactile, the physical forms of the city. The title of the first book is derived from oral folklore, while that of the latter refers to a dance form, the *pavane*. *Tres Tristes Tigres* favors dialogue and music, while *La Habana* stresses action and movement over the oral. *La Habana* is the film as "viewed" by the reader, and the author himself asserts that "es

---

[3] Josefina Ludmer, "*Tres Tristes Tigres*: Ordenes literarios y jerarquías sociales," *Revista Iberoamericana*, 45 (1979), 499.

exactamente eso: la lectura como un acto voyeurista. No pasa de noche como *Tres Tristes Tigres*, sino entre el día y el crepúsculo del cine" (8— September 1979). While *Tres Triste Tigres* invites the reader to join in his celebration of the spoken word, *La Habana* intimates a more passive role for the reader, that of a movie-goer.

Here we have the city of Havana seen through the eyes of an un-named first person narrator who at one point identifies himself as a movie camera (p. 537). The fact that *La Habana* is a book which would rather be a movie bespeaks its espousal to the carnivalesque on several counts. In its popular appeal and universal accessibility, the cinema is a modern-day equivalent of the carnival square. Even on a technical plane, the illusion of movement realized in film art through a continual flickering of light and shadow strongly suggests the focus on the present and the celebration of perpetual change in carnival.

A good part of *La Habana* takes place in movie theatres, essentially meeting houses or carnival squares where all types of people con-verge to participate in vicarious sensual experiences on the silver screen. In "Amor trompero" the narrator identifies himself as a Don Juan "burlado" and recounts experiences in which he combined his "amor fugaz" for women with his eternal passion for the cinema. He becomes now and again "un cateador, un rascabucheador, un tocador de damas en los cines" (p. 176). Although he never learns their names, he gives some of them nick-names such as "mi Everest por conquistar," and he is known to have followed some girls out of the theatre to their homes. He claims to have been looking for love, not just mere contact, in these "sesiones espiritistas eróticas" (p. 191). Numerous techniques are developed for this activity, but when he goes to the Lara Theatre, he must develop self-defense tactics against aggressive homosexuals and child molesters who are among the regular clientele. One time the "pirata pícaro" is injured by a cruel young woman who sticks him in the arm with a pin as he leans toward her. His only revenge is to compare her with female assassins in the movies. The chapter ends with an interlude in the cinema beside an anonymous woman who turns out to be a cook on her afternoon off.

Since this entire chapter centers on adventures in movie theatres, it is only natural that some of the narrator's views on the cinema emerge here: "(siempre los acontecimientos en la pantalla ocurrían, nunca eran contados, el relato superado por la ocurrencia)" (p. 207). This "aside," for example, seems to show a preference for the cinema over literature, an echo from Silvestre in *Tres Tristes Tigres*. On two other occasions the narrator makes explicit reference to an opinion shared by G. Caín in *Un oficio del siglo XX* and again by Silvestre in *Tres Tristes Tigres*: what happens on the movie screen is more real to him than the three-dimensional reality in color of everyday life. In other words, "los seres eran las sombras" (p. 224). The narrator's comprehension of a real-life situation, such as his wife's going into labor, is made possible only because of its similarity to an event he had seen in the movies.

Given that cinematic techniques are completely integrated into the narrator's *modus operandi*, the inner dialogue can easily be viewed as the coordinated efforts of the camera eye and the camera operator who guides the lens and shifts from present to past and from points in the past to the future. The cinematic analogy is especially adequate when the emphasis is on the visual over and above the temporal, such as when the narrator in love is describing the sky. Here the writer insists on the spatialization or the objectification of time and memory: "(Puedo seguir... haciendo del tiempo paisaje, no pasaje, pero prefiero hablar de la carne hecha verba)" (p. 337). At times memories evoke other memories and function as a "match cut" in the cinema. The mention of a taxi ride in the narration evokes the memory of a taxi ride in the earlier past in the *pueblo*. Points in space may similarly evoke memories at different points in time. When sitting on the wall of the Malecón with Dulce, for example, the narrator recalls the many other times since 1941 when he sat there with others. While admiring Margarita's legs he effects another "match cut" by referring, in parentheses, to the legs and ankles of a woman whom he had not yet met, and apparently does not meet until sometime after the events recounted in *La Habana* (p. 550).

As is often the case in the cinema, confusion in temporal chronology underscores the fact that the novel's progression is thematic and spatial rather than temporal. Not only are some of the chapters concurrent or overlapping in time, but the chronology within a chapter is occasionally jumbled as well. Physical locations and entities are described, but the episodes are separate and not linked by any transitional passages which might clarify exactly when certain events took place with respect to the chronology of other events. Although Juan Blanco is introduced in the final pages of "La casa de las transfiguraciones," he is nevertheless unknown to the narrator in the fifth chapter: "Juan Blanco...no era entonces un hombre sino un nombre" (p. 308). We are made aware that this particular episode of "Todo vence al amor" actually took place before the end of the first chapter. Our consternation may be alleviated by such explanatory notes as "Tal vez no fuera exacto en una cronología pero lo es en mi memoria que mide mi tiempo" (p. 288) or "el tiempo es elástico" (p. 326).

II

On the front cover of the book a street-photographer and an outmoded camera are shown in a central plaza in Havana. On the back cover a blank space next to the author's photograph suggests a movie screen where the contents of the book will be replayed in the author's memory. Between the covers is a "continous showing" of Havana viewed in its physical ambience through the roving photographic eyes of the narrator. Streets, buildings, parks and neighborhoods are named and located in terms of their proximity to some thirty-five movie theatres of the city and its environs: "El personaje es como siempre, obsesivo que soy, La Habana" (3 February 1979).

The first chapter is Havana viewed from within a *casa solariega*, a tenement house of sorts, located at Zulueta 408. The narrator is a child when he arrives in Havana and in "La casa de las transfiguraciones" he makes three basic discoveries: the city of Havana as an adventure, the language of Havana as distinguished from that of the *pueblo*, and sex. Havana holds many surprises in store for this uninitiated youth. The book opens with the boy of twelve years marveling over a beautiful marble staircase. His first stairway impresses him so much that it becomes a motif remindful of the Dantesque ascent from the everyday world to the paradise of the silver screen:

> Estamos en aquella Habana de vieja película en blanco y negro...donde abundaban tanto las rubias...que eran la última escala de una ascensión hacia el paraíso plasmado en el blanco edénico del lienzo de la pantalla de un cine, tras rebasar la etapa intermedia de las escaramuzas amatorias y ascender, por la vía purgativa, desde el infierno o subterráneo de la vida cotidiana en los barrios populares.[4]

---

[4] This quote is from Seix Barral / Biblioteca Breve's announcement of *La Habana Para Un Infante Difunto*.

In the family's second dwelling, Monte 822, the staircase is spiral and made of steel. In the later chapters, which extend outward in space and time from "La casa de las transfiguraciones," stairways are still noticed, but take second place to the women climbing them.

Some other aspects of the city which hold the young narrator in awe are the lights, the smells, the red light district, "la pila," "las pandillas" and continuous showings at the movies. The latter so impress him that he refers to the day of discovery as "Ese domingo de velaciones y revelaciones" (p. 29). In the *pueblo* it was not uncommon for a film to be interrupted or even terminated due to an electrical failure. The occasional circus in the town becomes the zoo in the city. The city is characterized by delights and wonders, but also by the hardships of poverty and the horrors of crime. The neighborhoods on the hills are poor in the *pueblo*, but well-off in Havana.

From his first tour on Eloy Santos' bus to his countless travels walking down the streets of Havana, the narrator names *barrios*, streets, parks, markets, movie theatres, schools, libraries, hotels, clubs, cafés and bus routes. With a street plan of Havana, one could fill in all the locales frequented or passed by in the narrator's endless chasing after women in Havana.

The city seems to have a vocabulary of its own, as well as differing customs: "la ciudad hablaba otra lengua, la pobreza tenía otro lenguaje" (p. 12). A few examples of these contrasts made by the narrator are:

En La Habana	En el pueblo	page
maricón	cundango	42
mariconería	cundanguería	42
cocinas y baños colectivos	... individuales o familiares	52
escaparate	armario	60
coqueta	consola tocador	60
queridas	amantes	62
todo judío llamado polaco	todo libanés y sirio llamado moro	85
pipo	padre	100
el piropo	el amor se iba en miradas	175
hasta luego	adiós	459
En el cine		
la tertulia	el paraíso o el gallinero	184
poner una película	dar una película	184

Some of the vocabulary the young narrator finds to be expressly *habanero* is, for example, "guagua," "quemar," "apearse," "los bayus" and the "medianoche" sandwich. In the *pueblo* one usually said "por favor," and "si, señor," whereas people look at the narrator strangely if he is that polite in the city.

The "story line" in *La Habana* progresses from descriptions and fantasies "del sexo en el solar" (p. 94), to platonic love, rites of passage and sexual relationships. In them, he passes through many levels of erotic involvement with women in his quest for happiness. For now, we will follow the camera eye to a few of "los cuartos carnales" (p. 166) of Zulueta 408, our narrator's home for eight years, to catch a glimpse of the child's world and his discovery of sex. In the author's words, *La Habana* "es una falsa memoria, los personajes son reducidos a cuerpos, a recuerdos carnales, confusos objetos del deseo" (18 November 1978).

As we are taken from room to room we meet friends and relatives from the *pueblo* who have come to visit or live in the city, people of all colors and walks of life: Chinese, Polish, Black, mulatto, Spanish. There is a barber, an organist, a ticket-taker and a "doctor" who has the only telephone in the building. The telephone, it seems, is used for indiscreet purposes, "Amor por control remoto" (p. 133). The "colonia sexual" (p. 119) contains prostitutes, a gigolo, a "kept" woman, a woman with a lover and two entire floors of homosexuals and lesbians of all ages. In this "escuela de escándalos" the sexual imagination of the child runs wild.

Fourteen year-old Emilia gives the narrator his first adult kiss. Her characterization consists of a physical portrait, for she, like most of the women in the book, has very few dialogue lines. "Emilia era muy reservada: hasta tenía los labios finos de los reservados, ...Emilia, delgada y pálida" (p. 53). The fact that her skin is lighter than that of her two sisters provides the narrator with an opportunity to digress on a related topic, "el culto a la mulata" (p. 51).

His second love in the building is Chelo, "sonriendo con su boca sensual, aumentada al morderse siempre ella el labio inferior y sus grandes ojos negros, rodeados de unas eternas ojeras malvas—que eran como el labio inferior de su mirada—y el pelo lacio cayéndole sobre la cara larga" (p. 137). In retrospect he believes he fell in love with Chelo because she resembled Ann Dvorak in the film *Caracortada*. His third love, Rosita, on the other hand, is the incarnation of a literary figure, Madame de Marelle. Other women, too, are compared to literary or film figures, Elvira with María Félix, and Lucinda with María Montez.

Several of the "older" women fascinate the youth as well, especially Severa, about twenty-seven, whom he describes as "muy habanera," with a character which is admirable and typical of many Cuban women:

> Consiste en una agresividad casi masculina, ... muy liberal con las malas palabras y tenía un sentido del humor agudo pero vulgar, eso que se llamó relajo, ... bordeando el tema erótico, cuando no cayendo en la pornografía, al mismo tiempo que insinúa la falta de respeto a todo (pp. 144-45).

During the epoch in which the narrator is courting Severa's niece, Rosita, his last love at Zulueta 408, the aunt surprises him on the balcony with an embrace from behind. This enigmatic occurrence causes him to greet his young Rosita with indifference from that day on. In a section devoted to the *calientapollas* he knew, we find an illustration of the *solar* as a place where "lo inimaginable era lo cotidiano" (p. 134). After a full page which describes Lucinda's physical attributes, or lack of them, the narrator defines his "labores literarias" as a "locutor libidinoso" for his "Mona Licenciosa." Lucinda asks him to read "novelitas" to her, which they do in secrecy, achieving thereby "el contacto sexual por las palabras" (p. 161).

In "La casa de las transfiguraciones" characterization is limited to very brief *estampas* of the carnal memories which provide the materials of the youth's sexual fantasies. Although the relationships with women begin to expand in the later chapters, flat characterization is essentially the norm, and is achieved by using types which are easily caricatured: maids, prostitutes, students, actresses and so on. Even the narrator is not well-rounded, for he insists on exploring only one dimension of his personality, his Donjuanesque search for happiness. A common element of Menippean satire is precisely that sort of limiting of the work to the treatment of a single idea, in this case erotic love, as an adventure. In the author's words, "El libro está narrado por un niño que termina de serlo al llegar a la ciudad, por un adolescente que encuentra a la ciudad y por un adulto que la adopta como suya.... Es la versión habanera de 'Don Juan en el infierno'" (New York University, 17 April 1980).

The theme of masturbation, introduced early in the book with reference to the *Satyricon* and *Memorias de una princesa rusa*, culminates in the two page masturbatory chapter "Amor propio," which is included at this point to provide a thematic transition between "La casa de las transfiguraciones" and the remainder of the book. The characters of "La casa..." inhabit the narrator's sexual fantasies and are, as is the *solar* itself, objectifications of his own inner being. The characters in the remaining chapters belong to the world outside and are more than just extensions of the narrator's personality. "Amor propio" intimates that eroticism progresses from fantasies to self-love before it can be experienced with others, that only after accepting oneself does the rest of the world become interesting. From this point on, the narrator begins to move outside the walls of Zulueta 408:

> Si una ventaja tenía Zulueta 408, aparte de la promiscuidad promisora, era estar en lo que era el centro de La Habana entonces y vivíamos rodeados de cines, aparte de otros espectáculos como el teatro de la vida, la comedia humana y así había poco pan pero cientos de circos (p. 202).

While the narrator insists on staying close to his central theme at all times, a richness of character shines through despite these "efforts." We get to know the narrator as both character and writer, and as his relationships with others deepen, some of the other characters, as well, take on more personality. Nonetheless, characterization of the types found in *La Habana* are developed strictly in terms of their interaction with the narrator as a character.

By the fifth chapter it becomes clear that the minor personages are being described not only through type-casting and physical description, but also by their use of language. "Todo vence al amor" tells the story of three failures in love during the narrator's school days. Carmina, a conservatory student, imitates Hedy Lamarr's hair style and is rather *cursi*. Her trademarks are "besos marcados en pañuelos y malapropismos en su boca" (p. 279). Virginia, a young divorcée who reads Baudelaire in the library, juxtaposes literary words with slang, such as "sugerir" with "guagua," while sitting on a park bench. She may read French literature, but she lives in Havana. Both Carmina and Virginia are lost to other men. Beba Far, a real beauty, becomes a female Narcissus and is lost to schizophrenia. While standing on the balcony at a party, she says something which recalls *Tres Tristes Tigres*: "Mira a Venus, el lucero del alba" (p. 312), mistaking a light bulb for a planet. In *Tres Tristes Tigres* it is Cué who is shown a dirty light bulb as the morning star. In *La Habana* it is the narrator.

This reference supports my hypothesis of the double in *Tres Tristes Tigres*, for it suggests the equation of Cué with the narrator of *La Habana*.

The ensuing chapters contain delightful stories of growing up in Havana. Julieta, "diosa del deseo" (p. 384), initiates the narrator in sex, while Dulce provides him with his first extended sexual relationship without guilt. The physical description of Dulce includes comparisons between her and cinema stars: "Usaba los labios dibujados a la manera de los finales de los años cuarenta, que eran los plenos cuarenta en el cine.... Si su boca recordaba a Joan Crawford, su nariz...era casi exacta a la nariz de Marlene Dietrich" (p. 428). Like all the women in *La Habana,* Dulce is a sexual object and the narrator remembers her more for her looks than for her conversation.

In "Casuales encuentros forzados" we find a portrait of the epitome of the *criaditas* for whom the narrator feels an occasional attraction. Her body is not exceptional, but the strange way she varies her speech from popular expressions and *dejo habanero* to clearly enunciated, passionate statements, shocks and amazes the narrator. A line taken directly from *La Novela del Aire*, such as "Tienes que jurarme amor eterno o no conseguirás seducirme, Rodolfo" (p. 514) is followed by something like: "¿Mi chino me quiere ver encuerá?" (p. 516). *La criadita* borrows not only her sentiments but also her language from radio soap operas.

The last main chapter, "La Amazona," begins when the narrator still lives at Zulueta 408, providing spatial and temporal continuity with the earlier chapters. He frequents theatrical groups and it is there that he first sees the woman who becomes the central figure in this long section. It is not until years later, after he is married, that their relationship actually begins. She is an actress with big green eyes, a woman with whom he believes he is in love for the first time. More mature than the other women he has known, she has been married, successful in her career and lived in Venezuela for awhile. Violeta del Valle tells him her "real" name, Margarita del Campo, on their first date.

The love relationship between Margarita and the narrator is the most passionate and involved of all those in the book, and it deserves further analysis. Both parties take each other and the relationship seriously, yet they interact, for the most part, as hunter and huntress. Pervading their interactions are animal instincts and possessiveness. The narrator's constant dictum is: "El que la sigue la mata"

(p. 531). He conceives of himself as a fox, a blend of "timidez, astucia y audacia" (p. 533), but he feels jealousy and expresses possessiveness. Margarita has many characteristics reminiscent of the legendary Amazons: she has but one breast, aborts a child and is independent, leaving two men, the last one for her career. Her possessiveness finds expression in violent acts, such as cutting her lover's hand with her fingernail so that he will never forget her. She also prepares a "poisonous" drink for him, for she enjoys wreaking vengeance on men by watching them suffer and die.

For the first time since he has been chasing women the narrator becomes emotionally involved. He has finally met someone who matters to him and who is capable of leaving her mark on him. Thus we have the hilarious vision of the narrator wearing a tee-shirt and a scarf about his neck on the hottest of summer days in order to cover Margarita's passion marks on his body. When the narrator refuses to leave Havana with her, she, in a style befitting her Amazonian image, departs with another woman.

Interestingly enough, Margarita is the only female the narrator seems to respect as a person, and it is she who shares, to a certain extent, his voyeuristic tendencies. The voyeuristic theme, which is exploited in the chapter called "La visión de un mirón miope," is central to the novel. The character-narrator here revels in his "mirada táctil" (p. 410) as he observes "cuerpos celestes" (p. 414) during late night vigils with a pair of binoculars. The same occurs for the reader of the book, as the narrator draws him into "la lectura como un acto voyeurista." Another parallel can be drawn along these same lines. The character-narrator goes to the movies, and at times watches them, while the reader "views" the book as if it were a serial movie, or a film of vignettes on a theme. Margarita exhibits a proneness to voyeurism and is capable of a "desdoblamiento de actriz y espectadora" (p. 575) in love-making. She is a "mirona...Escoptofílica de dipsómanos" (p. 606), while she enjoys watching him drink a special potion. The two are a near-match in their proclivity for name changes. The narrator is given three different names for his lover, and still he does not believe she has actually told him her real name. And yet, the narrator himself admits to having used as many as five pseudonyms.

The fact that Margarita has green eyes serves as a unifying theme in the book, as well as a haunting closing to the affair and the chapter. A reference to the green eyes of a beautiful leopard is the first appearance of this motif. It reappears in the mention of a popular myth surrounding the beauty of a dark-skinned woman with green eyes, and their manifestation in several women. As a child the narrator first experienced love and jealousy with his green-eyed cousin of six years. It is only twenty years later that the intensity of these emotions is repeated with the green-eyed Margarita. The uncanny resolution of his love for the legendary green-eyed women is in the birth of his daugher, born with teeth and green eyes.

The narrator synthesizes his knowledge of women in this last part of the book, making comparisons between the more important or outstanding women he has known to date. He reflects, for example, on the "matices de pronunciación femenina" (p. 553), comparing and contrasting the pronunciation of s's and c's by Julieta, Dulce, la criadita, his wife and Margarita. Dulce and Julieta are repeatedly compared to Margarita with regard to such traits as the inflection of their voices and the manias which he claims kept them distanced from a close relationship with him: Julieta's didacticism, Dulce's hypocrisy and his wife's hysteria. His wife fares well in a comparison of profiles, but her expression of pain during childbirth "Era como una versión desesperada de Julieta haciendo el amor a la francesa" (p. 671). One time he falls for a Hungarian telephone operator, partly because of her low, cultivated voice. While they are making out in the balcony of the theatre the passionate Don Juan bites her bare shoulder. He hears a crack and realizes that he has broken his false front teeth: "No eran dientes eróticos" (p. 527).

III

In order to unfold the nature of the narrator as writer we must analyze his inner dialogue, his parodic style and his relationship with the reader. While in *Tres Tristes Tigres* the main dialogue is between two characters, Silvestre and his co-writer and double, Cué, in *La Habana* this posture is singularly limited to an inner dialogue between two voices of the self-conscious "I," respectively the narrator and the writer, both of whom have access to the author's memories. In terms of menippea, this reflects the "dialogical attitude of man to himself," a sub-category of "moral psychological experimentation," which Bakhtin signals as a precursor of the split personality or doubles theme in modern literature. Cabrera Infante has described the infrastructure of *La Habana* as follows:

> ...el autor se desdobla en un narrador no omnisciente pero sí
> que es capaz de recordarlo todo, a veces con ira, a veces con
> ironía. El Narrador (innombrado) es por supuesto un alter ego
> del autor, un doble del escritor y mientras el Narrador recuerda
> su vida, el escritor la va reconstruyendo y a veces uno corrige al
> otro, el escritor pasando a ser un censor nemotécnico (8 Sep-
> tember 1979).

Throughout *La Habana*, the reader is given the impression that
comments written in parentheses are made by the writer, correcting
the narrator in his choice of words relative to the time of which he is
speaking. Cabrera Infante's success in maintaining a distinction
between narrator and writer is exemplified in this excerpt:

> Por lo menos en el cuarto del solar (estoy adelantándome
> lingüísticamente: en mi vocabulario todavía no existía la palabra
> solar: ya me he adelantado antes, pero era la introducción,
> mientras que ahora estamos in medias res) dormíamos en dos
> camas (p. 25).

The writer clarifies expressions used by the narrator: "en una palabra
(que siempre quiere decir más de una frase)" (p. 148), and justifies his
use of obscenities: "Carajo (usualmente destesto [sic] las obscenidades
pero cuando las empleo es que las otras palabras no sirven para nada:
donde mueren las palabras, nacen las malas palabras)" (p. 473). In
essence he provides explanatory notes on the narration, occasionally
correcting temporal references: "Ella tenía entonces (mejor debía
decir todavía)" (p. 62), and other times helping to remember details
that the narrator forgot: "(olvidé mencionar la revista más revela-
dora: *Esquire*...)" (p. 63). The comments within parentheses tend
towards linguistic concerns, word usage; in short, the writer's comments on the narration:

> ...apropincuarlas (dice el diccionario, ese cementerio de ele-
> fantes lingüísticos a donde van a morir las palabras, que esta
> palabra no se usa más que en sentido festivo, pero en mi pueblo
> era muy claro su sentido: arrimarse con segundas intenciones,
> que en mi caso, en esta época de mi vida, eran las primeras) (p.
> 195).

Besides providing etymological digressions, the writer's statements
often add greater depth and humor to the narration, as when he
describes his technique of telescoping time, or when, on numerous
occasions, he winds his way back and forth through the labyrinth of

time and memories. These include mixtures of verbal tenses, contrasting the "then" and the "now," differentiating between temporal and spatial references, and pointing out contrasts in knowledge and awareness of the narrator with regard to the epoch to which he is referring.

In a book which may be construed as autobiographical fiction, these sporadic and seemingly whimsical appearances by the writer cause our focus to shift from the past, back to the present, as "Cabrera Infante maintains a dialogue with his own past."[5] From the reader's perspective the writer pops in and out, receding ever again behind his typewriter ribbon. Meanwhile, the narrator, unaware of the intrusions, continues his story. While the writer must keep out of sight to satisfy minimally the conventions of fiction, his jack-in-the-box appearances provide distance, detachment and irony for the reader.

As in *Tres Tristes Tigres*, the narrator often confuses the reader with a mixture of verb tenses, to the extent that we become disoriented and painfully aware of his process of recounting the past. For the most part, the narrator uses the preterite and imperfect tenses to describe his experiences as a youth in Havana. Occasionally, however, he throws in temporal references which seem out of place in the midst of verbs in the past tense, such as "hasta ahora." In the process of referring to an event which lies in the future of the past story, and yet is still in the narrator's past, a switch to the present tense to establish the ambience of "la cultura del presente entonces" (p. 60) is jarring to the reader:

> Ortega me encargó la crítica de cine, que fue durante años mi profesión de fe—pero eso queda en el futuro. En el presente están los libros prestados esa tarde y mi salida de su casa—debió de ser un sábado, estoy seguro de que fue un sábado... (p. 218).

The narrator often makes us aware of different levels of time: "—pero ese recuerdo pertence al futuro y ahora hablo del presente, es decir del pasado" (p. 236). The effect is humorous when the writer uses his ominiscience to retroactively affect the behavior of the narrator as adolescent:

---

[5] Raymond D. Souza, in his review of *La Habana* in *Cuban Studies*, 11, 1 (1981), p. 96.

Me senté correctamente (recordé con presciencia las lecciones
que me dará un día un profesor de cinematografía, ... acerca de
cómo había que sentarse en el cine...) y obligué con mi acción
reparadora a que mi compañera abandonara el abrazo amoroso
y se sentara con corrección en su asiento (p. 231).

Our narrator uses temporal contrasts to compare his level of knowledge and awareness in the past with that of the present:

—¿Qué te parece Baudelaire?—me preguntó. Hoy podría decirle:
"Me interesa más su carnal Nadar" y salir así del paso de tan
tremenda pregunta. Entonces le dije la verdad, ... —No lo he
leído (p. 271).

And later, after more comments on Baudelaire and Virginia's interpretation of the poet: "Estas son, por supuesto, reflexiones actuales,
entonces sólo pensaba en llegar al parque" (p. 280). The writer adds
comments on a change in taste between "then" and "now": "(hoy día
las encontraría gordas pero entonces me parecían perfectas)" (p. 306).
He also notes his greater capacity for understanding and appreciation
of life today as compared with then: "(...pero esos datos...no me
pasaban por la mente entonces disfrutando como estoy...)" (p. 230).

While *La Habana* does not deal with literary parody on the grand
scale that *Tres Tristes Tigres* does, the book "está plagado de alitera-
ciones, parodias de frases hechas y por hacer y puns" (8 September
1979). Indeed, the most predominant stylistic device in *La Habana* is
the use of alliteration, especially in groupings of threes, for example:
"duros domos dorados" (p. 78), "su verticalidad me dio vértigo
invertido" (p. 34), "sola sombra sólida" (p. 54), "atónito ante el ataque"
(p. 54). For Cabrera Infante, by his own admission, alliteration is a
literary way of representing sexual acts: "Erotismo del cuerpo en el
recuerdo, erotismo de la palabra en la escritura."[6] The erotic aspect of
alliteration may be due to the linking of words by similar sounds, a
coming together, or the suggestion of a *ménage a trois*. There are
countless light-hearted parodies of famous phrases from literary and
cinematic works interwoven in the narration. The celebrated phrase
of Mallarmé, "Un coup de dés n'abolirá jamais le hasard," is found
several times in *La Habana* with variations: "Un golpe de faros nunca
abolirá el pesar" (p. 599). Lorca and Mallea appear together in an
alliterative parody: "(...verde que te odio verde, verde de muerte,

[6] Seix Barral's announcement.

todo verdor perecedor)" (p. 608). And Ramón Sender is recalled in
"no era entonces un hombre sino un nombre" (p. 308).

In an aside, the narrator describes his literary tastes, stating that
he admires the vulgarity of the *Quijote*, Sterne, Dickens and Joyce.
The fact that "la vulgaridad viva" (p. 530) of the cinema and popular
culture in general have been elevated to the category of art reflects
the narrator's own preferences: "...no estoy escribiendo historia de
la cultura sino poniendo la vulgaridad en su sitio—que está muy cerca
de mi corazón" (p. 531). True to the topical and publicist quality of
Menippean satire, the narrator manages to parody several newspaper
articles on the heinous crime committed at Zulueta 408. By citing the
articles, he shows up the lack of imagination of the journalists' styles.
Each quote contains the adjective *macabro*.

An ambivalent or carnivalistic attitude is usually evoked by a
reversal in the normally accepted way of perceiving reality. A mixture of opposites like the sacred with the profane, or any such
oxymoronic construct, may be shocking or blasphemous and is an
essential characteristic of the menippea. In the right measure and
with the requisite sense of humor and detachment, these same
contrasting images may evoke laughter and enable man to glimpse
past the barrier of opposites to the paradise beyond.

> [The] use of lyrical rhetorical language for an indecent subject is
> common enough in literature, as is the use of elegant prose for
> erotic frivolities, but it was particularly used by the Latin
> Menippean satirists. This frank and glorious acceptance of the
> physical side of life is often called a Renaissance characteristic,
> but it is more important to see it as a modern link with the
> ancient world in Seneca and Petronius who were not trying to
> do "dirt on life," but who were aiming at a fairly sophisticated
> public in the empire.[7]

An example of this type of juxtaposition in *La Habana* occurs during
an erotic incident, when the explicit description of a sexual encounter
is interrupted by a long etymological digression on the gender of
Cuban words referring to the male and female sexual members. The
writer is disconcerted by the fact that feminine nouns are used for
the male sexual organs and masculine nouns are used respectively for

---

[7] Dorothy Gabe Coleman, *Rabelais* (London: Cambridge University
Press, 1971), p. 99.

the females'. This combination of street language and erudite style, so typical of the *Satyricon*, is decidedly humorous.

Along with his "safari sexual" (p. 559) the narrator occasionally expresses concern with regard to the function of memory and remembering. The writer's "crónica de amores" (p. 401) is also "una retahíla de recuerdos" (p. 440). He believes that there is a logic in remembering which differs from everyday logic, for memories, like dreams and the theatre, may be imaginary:

> (la memoria es una traductora simultánea que interpreta los recuerdos al azar o siguiendo un orden arbitrario: nadie puede manipular el recuerdo y quien crea que puede es aquel que está más a merced del arbitrio de la memoria) (p. 520).

Forgetting and remembering are equated: "...sólo se recuerda lo que está olvidado" (p. 504). Perhaps by conveniently forgetting some memories, the narrator avoids having to tell all his secrets. After all, there are potential betrayals involved in remembering. "El recuerdo," for instance, is capable of deceiving "a la memoria," the narrator's "memoria" may betray him as a person, and remembering betrays words, "Las palabras, ahora, muertas, horizontales por el recuerdo..." (p. 599), as it becomes more and more difficult to recall their sounds. *La Habana*, twelve years after *Tres Tristes Tigres*, is written in Spanish, not Cuban.[8] Memories may be within memories, like the concentric circles of life at Zulueta 408. One memory evokes a former memory: "(nostalgia en la nostalgia, ese recuerdo entre estos recuerdos)" (p. 22). Some memories cause the narrator to be captivated by a Chinese girl who reminds him of Delia of Zulueta 408. Others revive memories which do not pertain to *La Habana*, but will be recorded in another book someday. Although uncertain, the narrator expresses an inclination to believe that memory and remembering provide a route to eternity not offered by life itself: "¿será que la memoria es imperecedera, que no lo es la vida, que el recuerdo puede salvar de la muerte?" (p. 595).

---

[8] Cabrera Infante at New York University. While *Tres Tristes Tigres* tries to capture the spoken language of Havana, including its dialects and idiosyncrasies, *La Habana* plays with the Spanish language and is more oriented toward the visual than the auditory. While *Tres Tristes Tigres* is a communal book, meant to be read aloud, *La Habana* provides a more solitary experience for the reader.

Perhaps the narrator has hopes for his own eternal existence through the relationship he establishes with the reader. As in *Tristram Shandy* and *Tres Tristes Tigres*, the narrator of *La Habana* carries on a dialogue with the reader, sometimes addressed as *tú* or *lector* but more often as *ustedes*. The first person narration tends to create the ambience of a dialogue with the readers even without specific reference to the latter: "Aunque objeto el ir y venir de algunas memorias modernas tanto como detesto la estricta cronología, hay una ocurrencia que tuvo lugar antes" (p. 113). This is especially the case when the narrator explains his stylistic oddities, such as having an exclamation mark only at the end of a sentence where he uses an oxymoron. The writer asks his readers to forget a certain phrase he uses, qualifying it as "una personificación torpe" (p. 402). He asks favors of them "(...hagan el favor de notarlo)" (p. 45), and even commands them "(No me pregunten cómo supe...)" (p. 407). The narrator, both as character and as writer, shares this familiarity with his readers, as the direct address to them is at times not in parentheses: "No sé si por esta página ya ustedes me conocen, pero si me conocieran sabrían que... (p. 389)," or "¿Alguno de ustedes, señoras y señores ha intentado...?" (p. 417). At other times it is inside parentheses: "(...También les pido que...)" (p. 402), or "(...permiso para una digresión...)" (p. 580). By engaging his readers in conversation, the narrator ensures not only the readers' involvement in the story, but the narrator's immortality as well. His reverence for memory suggests a belief that so long as he is remembered by someone, he will have achieved a certain kind of life beyond death.

IV

The Don Juan theme of erotic love in *La Habana*, complete with excursions into *machismo* and *marianismo*, may be viewed in its entirety as a ritual crowning and discrowning of the king of carnival. This performance represents, according to Bakhtin, "the very core of the carnivalistic attitude to the world—the pathos of vicissitudes and changes, of death and renewal" (p. 102). As a result of this alignment between the theme of *La Habana* and the carnivalesque, nearly all potential qualities of Menippean satire are to be found in *La Habana*. The most obvious, when speaking of the epilogue, is "experimental fantasticality," in Bakhtin's words, "...observation from an unusual point of view...coupled with radical changes in the scale of the observed phenomena" (p. 95). As usual, the author envisions the human condition as paradoxical. By ensuring his own and the reader's detachment, the comic element, as contrasted with the dogmatic, pervades all facets of the narrative.

Our narrator defines himself as a Don Juan, a libertine seducer of women, the prototype of the *macho* man in Spain and all of Latin America. Cabrera Infante writes: "Yo, como tantos hombres de mi generación, sufrimos la tensión del matriarcado en la casa y el machismo en la calle." In Cuba there is also the African heritage to take into consideration, which undoubtedly brings its own twist to the phenomenon of *machismo*. In *Tres Tristes Tigres* the rite of Sikán and Ekué is from the African all-male secret society Abakuá. Initiation rites consisted mainly of "pruebas de coraje—que eran muestras de machismo," and, "en su misterio central la mujer tiene la posición que el diablo en la religión cristiana" (30 June 1979).

While there are glaring examples of *machismo* in *La Habana*, the underlying tone of humor and parody renders it impossible to consider them a true indictment of the narrator as an insufferable *macho*. Although it is difficult not to interpret his role as such, the narrator's behavior must nonetheless be understood within the context of the societal norms which foster these patterns of *machismo* and *marianismo*. Margarita's sister, for example, is a widow because her husband was a victim of *machista* attitudes and behavior. When a stranger in the town uttered an obscene *piropo* to Atanasia, her husband had to defend his honor by fighting the verbal aggressor. As a result, he was killed instantly with a knife.

Our narrator is *machista* in his unfaithfulness to his wife, especially in "Casuales encuentros forzados," for seduction without emotional involvement is the trademark of Don Juan. The indifference shown to his wife's feelings is a manifestation of *machismo* that is counterbalanced by *marianismo*, the absolute rule of the woman in the home, along with her suffering and martyrdom. She lives in the folds of the family with other relatives who support her emotionally and help her rear the children. The sad result of this cultural pattern, declares Aniceto Aramoni, is that it is a vicious cycle in which neither men nor women achieve their due happiness.[9]

[9] Aniceto Aramoni, "Machismo," *Psychology Today*, January 1972, pp. 69-72.

The epigraph of *La Habana* is a line adopted from the film *King Kong*, in which an ape caricatures the *macho* image of strength, large genitals and the capacity to conquer women irregardless of their desires. At the height of his *machista* activities, the narrator finds himself to be a veritable King Kong. He is able to pick up nearly any girl he chooses, but on occasions he finds himself impotent after arriving at the *posada*. His relationship with Margarita practically cures the narrator of his former tendencies insofar as he cares to some extent about the woman with whom he is sleeping. In the epilogue the tables are turned in carnivalesque imagery, making a farce of the *macho* role pursued by the narrator. Now he is at the mercy of a "Queen Conga" who completely dominates the former Don Juan.

The reader is likely to feel confused by the particular way in which Cabrera Infante ends his book. We are, however, assured by Coleman that "whenever a reader is not sure what the author's attitude is or what reaction is expected from him we have irony with little satire.... [a] form of Menippean satire..." (Coleman, p. 105). During his talk at New York University, Cabrera Infante referred to his "Epílogo" by asking: "¿Qué ocurre cuando el hombre deja de pensar y se convierte en irracional?" The story was told to Cabrera Infante by his literary mentor Virgilio Piñera and is included in *La Habana* in homage to him.[10] Although the fantastic style of the epilogue comes as a shock at the close of a book which may be read as an autobiography or confession, the grotesque imagery of this popular story is reminiscent of Menippean satirists and carnival attitudes in general. The sequence contains several attributes central to the carnival attitude as defined by Bakhtin: "free, familiar contact among people," "eccentricity...[which] permits the latent sides of human nature to be revealed and developed in a concretely sensuous form," "carnivalistic mésalliances" and "profanation" (Bakhtin, p. 101).

The burlesque treatment of myth, another manifestation of Menippean satire, takes us to the end of *La Habana* and the consideration of the last word in the book's title: "Difunto." When the narrator enters the movie theatre in the epilogue, he is about to undergo a rite

---

[10] In "Vidas para leerlas," Cabrera Infante writes a fascinating dual biographical account of Virgilio Piñera and José Lezama Lima, comparing and contrasting the two writers. *Vuelta,* 4, No. 41 (April 1980), 4-16.

of passage, a veritable fantastic journey in the "paradise" section of
the theatre. In carnivalesque fashion, the book ends in a parody of
the adventures of a mythological hero and of anicent mythological
gods. In fact, the caricature of the gods resides in the pursued
woman's watching a cartoon of Pluto the Dog. Pluto, another name
for Hades, King of the Dead, inspires laughter in the woman (also
seen as a Terrible Mother or Fury) who, in the narrator's words, "Se
rió, se reía, se reirá para siempre, como una muñeca de carnaval" (p.
697). Her cosmic laughter is beyond good and evil and all other
polarizing forces to which mankind is usually subject. She has no fear
of death, for she is the goddess who creates, embraces and engulfs all
of life. Our mock-mythological hero must surmount certain obstacles
before he can cross the threshold into another spiritual realm. Instead
of the Clashing Rocks through which Jason sailed to reach a sea of
marvels, our narrator's dangerous pasage is between two cruel but
sensuous knees. The woman is seen as the quintessential goddess and
finally as Kali, whose title in Indian religion is "the Ferry Across the
Ocean of Existence."

Once having crossed the threshold, our narrator finds a sailor's
log book with the initials *AS*, which perhaps stand for *Agua Sagrada*, the
night sea, the water of the Underworld through which the hero must
pass. The Hindus believe that in death the soul must review and
assimilate the whole meaning of its past life. The narrator's falling
into an unknown sea represents Death, the stage during which he
relives his past life to learn its lessons; the sea also represents Life, in
preparation for rebirth at another level of existence. It is perhaps in
this timeless state that the narrator is recalling everyone and everything which has been related, as if the entire book were a "Dialogue
of the Dead." This is a style popularized by Lucian of Samosata (120
A.D.), who often includes Menippus and Pluto as central characters.
The narrator, like the mythological hero returning to normal life, is
daring and eccentric. He stuns and slays traditional literary dragons
with his genius. As he falls horizontally into an abyss, however, he
may already be experiencing rebirth, ready to start anew as the
infant at the beginning of the novel.

The Janus-like symbol of death and birth in carnival and mythological imagery reads as "the beginning in the end" in the cinematic
ending of *La Habana*. The narrator has indicated a belief in this
imagery at several points throughout the book. With reference to his

home at Zulueta 408, which provides the focal point of the novel, the location is defined as "nuestra meta, fin que era un eterno comienzo" (p. 60). Not only did the narrator live there several times, always returning to his first place of residence in Havana, but the reader as well returns repeatedly to this location in the visual odyssey of *La Habana*. Zulueta 408 is a microcosm, harboring its own secrets, like a book, a film, a human being. Returning to the epilogue, the narrator reflects: "Era mi voz al fin—o al principio" (p. 696), thus underlining his confusion of the beginning with the end, or equating the two. The volume closes with a phrase which draws together the erotic and cinematic themes with a flair matched only by Yorick at the end of *Tristram Shandy*. Cabrera Infante's narrator writes: "Aquí llegamos," suggesting that the episodes contained in the body of the book will be re-run *ad infinitum* on the reader's memory.

✣ Conclusion ✣

Characterization has often served as a focal point in this generic exploration into Cabrera Infante's literary province. As the means by which a writer attributes qualities or characteristics to the central figures of his work, be they people or objects, characters are fictional entities to which reader and author alike relate. In Cabrera Infante characterization is a function of Menippean satire, the literary tradition which best defines the essence of this author's works. The choice of genre, in this instance, is not a conscious one on the part of the author, who, although well-read in works within the Menippean tradition and aware of the characteristics of the genre, is nonetheless unaware of Menippean satire per se.[1] The author writes within one genre or another because of a personal affinity for that particular way of expressing himself. From the critic's perspective, then, it is most productive to approach Cabrera Infante's works with expectations and questions relevant to that genre.

Through my discussions of the *Satyricon* and *Tristram Shandy*, which

---

[1] This statement was confirmed in a conversation with Cabrera Infante at Yale University, 17 April 1980.

qualify as Menippean satire and novel, or a combination of the two, I have sought to clarify Cabrera Infante's early statements with regard to the importance of these works to his creation of *Tres Tristes Tigres*. As a version of the *Satyricon*, *Tres Tristes Tigres* inherits elements of Menippean satire and shares methods of characterization with Petronius' work. Both *Tres Tristes Tigres* and *La Habana* are narrated by characters related in spirit to Tristram, a first-person narrator whose nine volumes juxtapose erudition, caricature and parody. Other characteristics of Menippean satire which are present in varying degrees in the four works in question are characterization by "humor" or ruling passion, fragmentation or digression in the narrative, very little plot line (providing for an aura of suspense, uncertainty, ambiguity) and a comic element which pervades all levels of the works.

Cabrera Infante's major works are Menippean in their adherence to a single ideological issue, in *Tres Tristes Tigres* betrayal, and in *La Habana* erotic love. On the level of language, *Tres Tristes Tigres* exposes the conventions of language and literature as betraying the vitally experienced realities which they purport to express. Carlos Fuentes has suggested that many Latin American writers find that the Spanish language is not expansive enough to describe their reality, a world shaped by cultural and linguistic forces which are not exclusively Spanish.

Havana in the 1950's presented a *mélange* of such forces, represented especially by African and North American presences. Through a desire to share his particular awareness of this situation, and the limitations of language in general, Cabrera Infante makes the Spanish language burst at its seams, at once creating and destroying with his medium in anagrams, neologisms, alliteration, puns and parodies: "My ideal is absolute identity between reader and writer. If that is not entirely possible, I will accept gradation, but never degradation, of one or the other."[2]

The peculiar attitude toward language found in *Tres Tristes Tigres*, wherein the word itself becomes the material of literature, was originally a feature of Menippean satire, according to Bakhtin. *La Habana* maintains this spirit in its innovative utilization of language. Written at a greater distance from the Hispanic world from which it springs, *La Habana* is a funny treatise on *machismo*. In a sense exposing

---

[2] Rita Guibert, *Seven Voices* (New York: Knopf, 1973), p. 405.

and betraying an aspect of his cultural heritage, Cabrera Infante parodies *machismo*, showing it up as a comical phenomenon. In *La Habana* as in *Tres Tristes Tigres*, the light and comic nature of the reading belies an undercurrent of seriousness, yet another characteristic of serio-comic genres such as Menippean satire. Juxtapositions or "carnivalistic *mésalliances*" which unite "the sacred with the profane, the lofty with the lowly" (Bakhtin, p. 101), are the sort of images which provide the humor of incongruity so prevalent in these works.

If Cabrera Infante's writings are carnivalistic, formalized into language as Menippean satire, what then might we say is the ritual they seek to express? As in carnival, when the people mocked the gods in order to provoke them to change, to produce, to perform their duties, so too in Cabrera Infante's works language and the traditional novel form are mocked, abused and challenged in every way. Cabrera Infante's serio-comic literature celebrates change, perpetual motion, the life and death of language and the novel.[3] Language, as a symbol of man's rationality, is profaned and purified. The norms of the novel are nearly abolished, reminiscent of the upheaval of hierarchies and values in carnival juxtapositions. For new life the novel must laugh at itself, die and return to its origins in Menippean satire.

---

[3] Bakhtin uses the expression "jolly relativity" to describe the atmosphere of the carnival, in which change is celebrated and hierarchies are abolished. "All carnival symbols... include within themselves the perspective of negation (death), or its opposite. Birth is fraught with death, and death with new birth" (p. 101).

BIBLIOGRAPHY

A. GUILLERMO CABRERA INFANTE: Primary and Secondary Sources

Cabrera Infante, Guillermo. *Arcadia todas las noches*. Barcelona: Seix Barral, 1978.

————. "Epilogue for Late(nt) Readers." *Review 72* (Winter 1971-Spring 1972), 23-32.

————. *La Habana Para Un Infante Difunto*. Barcelona: Seix Barral, 1979.

————. *Tres Tristes Tigres*. Barcelona: Seix Barral, 1965.

————. *Un oficio del siglo XX: G. Caín 1954-60*. La Habana: Ediciones R, 1963; rpt. Barcelona: Seix Barral, 1973.

————. "Vidas para leerlas." *Vuelta*, 4, No. 41 (abril 1980), 4-16.

Alvarez-Borland, Isabel. *Discontinuidad y ruptura en G. Cabrera Infante*. Gaithersburg, Maryland: Ediciones Hispamérica, 1982.

Bensoussan, Albert. "Entrevistas: Guillermo Cabrera Infante." *Insula*, No. 286 (Sept. 1970), p. 4.

Carpenter, Jane F. "The Ontological Prison: Paradoxes of Perception in the Contemporary Latin American Novel." Diss. Cornell 1975.

Cozarinsky, Edgardo. "Páginas del libro de la noche: *Arcadia todas las noches*." *escandalar*, 3 (1980), 90-92.

Fuentes, Carlos. *La nueva novela hispanoamericana*. Mexico: Joaquin Mortiz, 1969.

Gallagher, D. P. "Guillermo Cabrera Infante." In *Modern Latin American Literature*. New York: Oxford University Press, 1973, pp. 164-85.

González, Eloy R., and Barbara Sanborn. "Universal Symbolism in *Tres Tristes Tigres*: The Spiral and the Circle." *Selecta*, 1 (1980), 98-101.

Goytisolo, Juan. "Lectura cervantina de *Tres Tristes Tigres*." *Revista Iberoamericana*, 42 (1976), 1-18.

Guibert, Rita. *Seven Voices: Seven Latin American Writers Talk to Rita Guibert*. Trans. Frances Partridge. New York: Alfred A. Knopf, 1973.

Jiménez, Reynaldo L. *Guillermo Cabrera Infante y Tres Tristes Tigres.* Miami: Ediciones Universal, 1977.

Kadir, Djelal. "Nostalgia or Nihilism: Pop Art and the New Spanish American Novel." *Journal of Spanish Studies: Twentieth Century,* 2 (1974), 127-35.

Levine, Suzanne Jill. "La escritura como traducción: *Tres Tristes Tigres* y una *Cobra.*" *Revista Iberoamericana,* 41 (1975), 557-67.

Little, William T. "Notas acerca de *Tres Tristes Tigres* de G. Cabrera Infante." *Revista Iberoamericana,* 36 (1970), 635-42.

Ludmer, Josefina. "*Tres Tristes Tigres*: Ordenes literarios y jerarquías sociales." *Revista Iberoamericana,* 45 (1979), 493-512.

MacAdam, Alfred J. "*Tres Tristes Tigres*: El vasto fragmento." *Revista Iberoamericana,* 41 (1975), 549-56.

Malcuzynski, M.-Pierrette. "*Tres tristes tigres,* or the Treacherous Play on Carnival." *Ideologies and Literature,* 3, No. 15 (1980).

Matas, Julio. "Orden y visión de *Tres Tristes Tigres.*" *Revista Iberoamericana,* 40 (1974), 87-104.

Merrim, Stephanie. "A Secret Idiom: The Grammar and Role of Language in *Tres Tristes Tigres.*" *Latin American Literary Review,* 8, No. 16 (1980), 96-116.

————. "*La Habana para un infante difunto* y su teoría topográfica de las formas." *Revista Iberoamericana,* 48 (1982), 403-13.

Mickelsen, Vicki Gillespie. "Games Novelists Play: Technical Experiments in *La Muerte de Artemio Cruz, La Casa Verde, Tres Tristes Tigres,* and *Rayuela.*" Diss. Indiana University 1974.

Mitchell, Phyllis. "The Reel Against the Real: Cinema in the Novels of Guillermo Cabrera Infante and Manuel Puig." *Latin American Literary Review,* 6 (1977), 22-29.

Prieto, Antonio. "*Tres Tristes Tigres*: El carnaval de la palabra." Thesis, Princeton University 1976.

Resnick, Claudia Cairo. "The Use of Jokes in Cabrera Infante's *Tres Tristes Tigres* [*Three Trapped Tigers*]." *Latin American Literary Review,* 4 (1976), 14-21.

Ríos, Julian, ed. *Guillermo Cabrera Infante.* Madrid: Editorial Fundamentos, 1974.

Rodríguez-Monegal, Emir. "Cabrera Infante: la novela como autobiografía total." *Revista Iberoamericana,* 47 (1981) 265-71.

————. "Estructura y significaciones de *Tres Tristes Tigres.*" *Sur,* 320 (1969), pp. 38-51.

————. "Las fuentes de la narración." *Mundo Nuevo,* No. 25 (1968), pp. 41-58.

————. "Los nuevos novelistas." *Mundo Nuevo,* No. 17 (1967), pp. 19-25.

Schraibman, José. "Cabrera Infante, tras la búsqueda del lenguaje." *Insula,* 286 (1970), pp. 1, 15, 16.

Siemens, William L. "Guillermo Cabrera Infante: Language and Creativity." Diss. University of Kansas, 1971.

————. "*Heilsgeschichte* and the Structure of *Tres Tristes Tigres.*" *Kentucky Romance Quarterly,* 22 (1975), 77-90.

————. "Mirrors and Metamorphosis: Lewis Carroll's Presence in *Tres tristes tigres.*" *Hispania,* 62 (1979), 297-303.

————. "Women as Cosmic Phenomena in *Tres Tristes Tigres.*" *Journal of Spanish Studies: Twentieth Century,* 3 (1975), 199-209.

Souza, Raymond D. "Cabrera Infante: Creation in Progress." In his *Major Cuban Novelists: Innovation and Tradition.* Columbia: University of Missouri Press, 1976, pp. 80-100.

Tittler, Jonathan. "Intratextual Distance in *Tres Tristes Tigres.*" *Modern Language Notes,* 93 (1978), 285-96.

Vázquez Older, Dora. "El juego contradictorio en Cabrera Infante." Diss. Brown 1977.

Volek, Emil. "*Tres tristes tigres* en la jaula verbal: las antinomias dialécticas y la tentativa de lo absoluto en la novela de Guillermo Cabrera Infante." *Revista Iberoamericana,* 47 (1981), 175-83.

B. PETRONIUS: Primary and Secondary Sources

Petronius. *Satyricon.* Trans. J. P. Sullivan. Penguin, 1974.

Abbott, Frank Frost. "Use of Language as a means of Characterization in Petronius." *Classical Philology,* 2 (1907), 43-50.

Arrowsmith, William. "Luxury and Death in the *Satyricon.*" *Arion,* 5, No. 3 (1966), 304-31.

————, trans. *Satyricon.* By Petronius. New York: Mentor, 1959.

Corbett, Philip B. *Petronius.* New York: Twayne, 1970.

Crum, Richard H. "Petronius and the Emperors; I: Allusions in the *Satyricon.*" *Classical Weekly,* 45, No. 11 (1952), 161-99.

George, Peter. "Style and Character in the *Satyricon.*" *Arion,* 5, No. 3 (1966), 336-58.

Highet, Gilbert. "Petronius the Moralist." *Transactions of the American Philosophical Association,* 72 (1941), 180-91.

Killeen, J. F. "James Joyce's Roman Prototype." *Comparative Literature,* 9 (1957), 193-203.

Rankin, H. D. *Petronius the Artist: Essays on the Satyricon and its Author.* The Hague: Martinus Nijhoff, 1971.

Rini, Anthony. "Popular Superstitions in Petronius and Italian Superstitions of To-Day." *Classical Weekly*, 22, No. 11 (Jan. 7, 1929), 83-86.

Rose, K. F. C. *The Date and Author of the "Satyricon."* Leiden: E. J. Brill, 1971.

————. "The Petronian Inquisition: An Auto-Da-Fe." *Arion*, 5, No. 3 (1966), 275-301.

Schnur, Harry C. "The Economic Background of the *Satyricon*." *Latomus*, 18 (1959), 790-99.

Steele, R. B. "Literary Adaptations and References in Petronius." *Classical Journal*, 15 (1920), 279-93.

Sullivan, J. P. *The Satyricon of Petronius: A Literary Study*. Bloomington: Indiana University Press, 1968.

Veyne, P. "Le 'Je' dans le *Satyricon*." *Revue des Etudes Latines*, 42 (1964), 301-23.

C. LAURENCE STERNE: Primary and Secondary Sources

Sterne, Laurence. *The Life and Opinions of Tristram Shandy, Gentleman*. Ed. Ian Watt. Boston: Houghton Mifflin, 1965.

Anderson, Howard. "*Tristram Shandy* and the Reader's Imagination." *PMLA*, 86 (1971), 966-73.

————. "A Version of Pastoral: Class and Society in *Tristram Shandy*." *Studies in English Literature*, 7 (1967), 509-29.

Baird, Theodore. "The Time-Scheme of *Tristram Shandy* and a Source." *PMLA*, 51 (1936), 803-20.

Booth, Wayne C. "Did Sterne Complete *Tristram Shandy*?" *Modern Philology*, 48 (1951), 172-83.

————. *The Rhetoric of Fiction*. Chicago: University of Chicago Press, 1961.

————. "The Self-Conscious Narrator in Comic Fiction before *Tristram Shandy*." *PMLA*, 67 (1952), 163-85.

Cash, Arthur H. "The Lockean Psychology of *Tristram Shandy*." *Journal of English Literary History*, 22 (1955), 125-35.

Drew, Elizabeth. *A Modern Guide to Fifteen English Masterpieces*. New York: W. W. Norton, 1963.

Evans, James E. "Tristram as Critic: Momus's Glass versus Hobby-Horse." *Philological Quarterly*, 50 (1971), 669-71.

Farrell, William J. "Nature Versus Art as a Comic Pattern in *Tristram Shandy*." *Journal of English Literary History*, 30 (1963), 16-35.

Faurot, Ruth Marie. "Mrs. Shandy Observed." *Studies in English Literature*, 10 (1970), 579-89.

Freedman, William. "*Tristram Shandy*: The Art of Literary Counterpoint." *Modern Language Quarterly*, 32 (1971), 268-80.

Griffin, Robert J. "Tristram Shandy and Language." *College English*, 23 (1961-62), 108-12.

Hartley, Lodwick. *Laurence Sterne in the Twentieth Century: An Essay and Bibliography of Sternean Studies 1900-1965*. Chapel Hill: University of North Carolina Press, 1966.

Hazlitt, William. *Lectures on the English Comic Writers*. Vol. VI of *Complete Works of William Hazlitt*. London: J. M. Dent and Sons, 1931.

Holtz, William V. *Image and Immortality: A Study of "Tristram Shandy"* Providence: Brown University Press, 1970.

James, Overton Philip. *The Relation of "Tristram Shandy" to the Life of Sterne*. The Hague: Mouton and Co., 1966.

Jefferson, D. W. "*Tristram Shandy* and the Tradition of Learned Wit." *Essays in Criticism*, I (1951), 225-48.

Kyle, Carol A. "A Note on Laurence Sterne and the Cannon-Bullet of John Locke." *Philological Quarterly*, 50 (1971), 672-74.

Laird, John. *Philosophical Incursions into English Literature*. New York: Russell and Russell, 1962.

Lehman, B. H. "Of Time, Personality, and the Author: A Study of *Tristram Shandy*: Comedy." *University of California Publications in English*, 8, No. 2 (1941), 233-50.

MacLean, Kenneth. *John Locke and English Literature of the Eighteenth Century*. New Haven: Yale University Press, 1936.

Maskell, Duke. "Locke and Sterne, or Can Philosophy Influence Literature?" *Essays in Criticism*, 23 (1973), 22-39.

McKillop, A. D. "Laurence Sterne." In *The Early Masters of English Fiction*. Lawrence: University of Kansas Press, 1956, pp. 182-219.

McMaster, Juliet. "Experience to Expression: Thematic Character Contrasts in *Tristram Shandy*." *Modern Language Quarterly*, 32 (1971), 42-57.

New, Melvyn. *Laurence Sterne as Satirist*. Gainesville: University of Florida Press, 1969.

Nuttall, A. D. *A Common Sky: Philosophy and the Literary Imagination*. London: Chatto and Windus for Sussex University Press, 1974.

Parish, Charles. "The Nature of Mr. Tristram Shandy, Author." *Boston University Studies in English*, 5 (1961), 74-90.

————. "The Shandy Bull Vindicated." *Modern Language Quarterly*, 31 (1970), 48-52.

Petrie, Graham. "Note on the Novel and the Film: Flashbacks in *Tristram Shandy* and *The Pawnbroker*." *Western Humanities Review*, 21 (1967), 165-69.

————. "Rhetoric as Fictional Technique in *Tristram Shandy.*" *Philological Quarterly*, 48 (1969), 479-94.

Piper, William Bowman. "Tristram Shandy's Digressive Artistry." *Studies in English Literature*, 1, No. 3 (1961), 65-76.

Russell, H. K. "*Tristram Shandy* and the Technique of the Novel." *Studies in Philology*, 42 (1945), 581-93.

Shklovsky, Victor. "Art as Technique: Sterne's *Tristram Shandy*: Stylistic Commentary." In *Russian Formalist Criticism: Four Essays*. Trans. Lee T. Lemon and Marion J. Reis. Lincoln: University of Nebraska Press, 1965, pp. 3-57.

Spacks, Patricia Ann Meyer. *Imagining a Self: Autobiography and Novel in Eighteenth-Century England*. Cambridge: Harvard University Press, 1976.

Stedmond, John M. *The Comic Art of Laurence Sterne: Convention and Innovation in "Tristram Shandy" and "A Sentimental Journey."* Toronto: University of Toronto Press, 1967.

Stewart, Jack F. "Romantic Theories of Humor Relating to Sterne." *The Personalist*, 49 (1968), 459-73.

Sutherland, James. "Some Aspects of Eighteenth-Century Prose." In *Essays on the Eighteenth Century Presented to David Nichol Smith*. Oxford, 1945, pp. 94-110.

Theobald, D. W. "Philosophy and Imagination: an Eighteenth-Century Example." *The Personalist*, 47 (1966), 315-27.

Towers, A. R. "Sterne's Cock and Bull Story." *Journal of English Literary History*, 24 (1957), 12-29.

Traugott, John, ed. *Laurence Sterne: A Collection of Critical Essays*. Englewood Cliffs, New Jersey: Prentice-Hall, 1968.

————. *Tristram Shandy's World: Sterne's Philosophical Rhetoric*. Berkeley: University of California Press, 1954.

Tuveson, Ernest. *The Imagination as a Means of Grace: Locke and the Aesthetics of Romanticism*. Berkeley: University of California Press, 1960.

————. "Locke and the Dissolution of the Ego." *Modern Philology*, 52 (1955), 159-74.

Van Ghent, Dorothy. "On *Tristram Shandy*." In *The English Novel: Form and Function*. Harper Torchbooks, 1961, pp. 83-98.

Wagoner, Mary S. "Satire of the Reader in *Tristram Shandy*." *Texas Studies in Literature and Language*, 8, No. 3 (1966), 337-44.

Watkins. W. C. B. *Perilous Balance: The Tragic Genius of Swift, Johnson, and Sterne*. Princeton: Princeton Unversity Press, 1939.

Watt, Ian. "The Comic Syntax of *Tristram Shandy*." In *Studies in Criticism and Aesthetics 1660-1800*. Eds. Howard Anderson and John S. Shea. Minneapolis: University of Minnesota Press, 1967, pp. 315-31.

————. "Realism and the Novel." *Essays in Criticism*, 2 (1952), 367-96.

Woolf, Virgina. *The Common Reader: Second Series.* London, 1932.

D. GENERAL

Allinson, Francis G. *Lucian: Satirist and Artist.* New York: Longmans, Green and Co., 1927.

Allott, Miriam. *Novelists on the Novel.* New York: Columbia University Press, 1959.

Apuleius. *The Golden Ass: Being the Metamorphoses of Lucius Apuleius.* Trans. W. Adlington. Cambridge: Harvard University Press, 1977.

Aramoni, Aniceto. "Machismo." *Psychology Today*, January 1972, pp. 69-72.

Bakhtin, Mikhail. *Problems of Dostoevsky's Poetics.* Trans. R. W. Rotsel. Ann Arbor: Ardis, 1973.

————. *Rabelais and His World.* Trans. Helene Iswolsky. Cambridge: The M. I. T. Press, 1968.

————. *The Dialogic Imagination: Four Essays by M. M. Bakhtin.* Ed. Michael Holquist. Trans. Caryl Emerson and Michael Holquist. Austin: University of Texas Press, 1981.

Baquero Goyanes, Mariano. *Estructuras de la Novela Actual.* 2nd ed. Barcelona: Planeta, 1972.

Blom, Eric, ed. *Grove's Dictionary of Music and Musicians.* 5th ed. New York: St. Martin's Press, 1955.

Campbell, Joseph. *The Hero With a Thousand Faces.* Princeton: Princeton University Press, 1972.

Coleman, Dorothy Gabe. *Rabelais: A Critical Study in Prose Fiction.* London: Cambridge University Press, 1971.

Davis, Robert Murray, ed. *The Novel: Modern Essays in Criticism.* Englewood Cliffs: Prentice-Hall, 1969.

De Rougemont, Denis. *Love Declared: Essays on the Myths of Love.* Trans. Richard Howard. New York: Random House, 1963.

Erikson, Erik H. *Identity: Youth and Crisis.* New York: W. W. Norton, 1968.

Fernández Moreno, Cesar, et. al. *América Latina en su Literatura.* México: Siglo veintiuno editores, 1972.

Forster, E. M. *Aspects of the Novel.* New York: Harcourt, 1927.

Frye Northrop. "The Four Forms of Prose Fiction." *Hudson Review*, 2 (1949-50), 582-95.

————. *Spiritus Mundi: Essays on Literature, Myth, and Society.* Bloomington: Indiana University Press, 1976.

Galsworthy, John. *The Creation of Character in Literature.* Oxford: Oxford University Press, 1931.

Gass, William H. *Fiction and the Figures of Life.* New York: Knopf, 1970.

Gillet, Joseph E. "The Autonomous Character in Spanish and European Literature." *Hispanic Review,* 24, No. 3 (1956), 179-90.

Goetschius, Percy. *The Structure of Music.* Westport, Conn.: Greenwood Press, 1970.

González Echevarría, Roberto. *Alejo Carpentier: The Pilgrim at Home.* Ithaca: Cornell University Press, 1977.

Hamilton, Edith. *Mythology: Timeless Tales of Gods and Heroes.* New York: New American Library, 1969.

Hardy, John Edward. *Man in the Modern Novel.* Seattle: University of Washington Press, 1964.

Harvey, W. J. *Character and the Novel.* Ithaca: Cornell University Press, 1965.

Keppler, Carl F. *The Literature of the Second Self.* Tucson: University of Arizona Press, 1972.

Langbaum, Robert. *The Mysteries of Identity.* New York: Oxford University Press, 1978.

Langer, Susanne K. *Philosophy in a New Key.* 3rd ed. Cambridge: Harvard University Press, 1971.

Lucian. *Selected Works.* Trans. Bryan P. Reardon. Indianapolis: Bobbs-Merrill, 1965.

MacAdam, Alfred J. "Northrop Frye's Theory of Genres and the New Literature of Latin America." *Revista Canadiense de Estudios Hispánicos,* 3 (1979), 287-90.

Mañach, Jorge. *Indagación del Choteo.* 3rd ed. Miami: Mnemosyne Publishing Co., 1969.

McCarthy, Barbara P. "Lucian and Menippus." *Yale Classical Studies,* 4 (1934), 3-55.

Mendilow, A. A. *Time and the Novel.* New York: Humanities Press, 1972.

Murdoch, Iris. "The Sublime and the Beautiful." *Yale Reivew,* 49 (1959), 247-71.

Potts, L. J. *Aristotle on the Art of Fiction.* Cambridge University Press, 1953.

Rabelais, François. *Gargantua and Pantagruel.* London: J. M. Dent and Sons, 1929. rpt. 1954.

Rank, Otto. *The Double: A Psychoanalytic Study.* Chapel Hill: University of North Carolina Press, 1971.

————. *The Myth of the Birth of the Hero and other Writings*. New York: Random House, 1964.

Rodríguez-Monegal, Emir. "Carnaval / Antropofagia / Parodia." *Revista Ibero-americana*, 45 (1979), 401-12.

Rogers, Robert. *A Psychoanalytic Study of the Double in Literature*. Detroit: Wayne State University Press, 1970.

Sarduy, Severo. *Barroco*. Buenos Aires: Editorial Sudamericana, 1974.

————. *Escrito sobre un cuerpo*. Buenos Aires: Editorial Sudamericana, 1969.

Sarraute, Nathalie. *The Age of Suspicion: Essays on the Novel*. Trans. Maria Jolas. New York: George Braziller, 1963.

Sartre, Jean-Paul. *Literary and Philosophical Essays*. Trans. Annette Michelson. New York: Collier Books, 1962.

Schwartz, Elias. "The Nature of Literary Genres." In *The Forms of Feeling*. London: Kennikat Press, 1972, pp. 72-92.

Seltzer, Alvin J. *Chaos in the Novel: The Novel in Chaos*. New York: Schocken Books, 1974.

Spiegel, Alan. *Fiction and the Camera Eye: Visual Consciousness in Film and the Modern Novel*. Charlottesville: Universtiy Press of Virginia, 1976.

Stambaugh, Joan. "Music as a Temporal Form." *Journal of Philosophy*, 61 (1964), 265-80.

Stevick, Philip. *The Theory of the Novel*. New York: Macmillan, 1967.

Taylor, Houghton W. "*Particular Character: An Early Phase of a Literary Evolution.*" *PMLA*, 60 (1945), 161-74.

Tieje, Arthur Jerrold. *The Theory of Characterization in Prose Fiction Prior to 1740*. Minneapolis: Bulletin of the University of Minnesota, 1916.

Tymms, Ralph. *Doubles in Literary Psychology*. Cambridge: Bowes and Bowes, 1949.

Von Franz, Marie-Louise. *A Psychological Interpretation of the Golden Ass of Apuleius*. New York: Spring Publication, 1970.

Walcutt, C. C. *Man's Changing Mask: Modes and Methods of Characterization in Fiction*. Minneapolis: University of Minnesota Press, 1966.

Waldeck, Peter B. *The Split Self from Goethe to Broch*. Lewisburg: Bucknell University Press, 1979.

Weiger, John G. *The Individuated Self: Cervantes and the Emergence of the Individual*. Athens: Ohio University Press, 1979.

Addendum to Bibliography follows on p. 124

Nelson, Ardis L. "El doble, el recuerdo, y la muerte: Elementos de fugacidad en la narrativa de G. Cabrera Infante." *Revista Iberoamericana*, 49 (1983), 509-21.

————. "*Tres tristes tigres* y el cine." *Kentucky Romance Quarterly*, 29 (1982), 391-404.

Shank, R. C. *Conceptual Information Processing.* North Holland, 1975.

Whorf, Benjamin Lee. *Language, Thought and Reality: Selected Writings.* Cambridge: Technology Press of Massachusetts Institute of Technology. 1956.